The Intelligent
Cat

GRACE POND, FZS *and*
ANGELA SAYER

The Intelligent
Cat

A Perigee Book

Perigee Books
are published by
G. P. Putnam's Sons
200 Madison Avenue
New York, New York 10016

This is an authorized reprint of a hardcover edition
originally published by The Dial Press/James Wade.

Originally published in Great Britain by
Davis-Poynter Limited, London.

Library of Congress Cataloging in Publication Data
Pond, Grace.
    The intelligent cat.

    Includes index.
    1. Cats—Behavior. 2. Cats—Psychology.
I. Sayer, Angela, joint author. II. Title.
[SF446.5.P66 1980]   636.8   79-20141
ISBN 0-399-50459-1

First Perigee Printing, 1980

PRINTED IN THE UNITED STATES OF AMERICA

Second Impression

Contents

Contents

The Intelligent Cat

Introduction to and History of the Domestic Cat

The lions, leopards, lynxes, pumas, tigers, Persians and the tabbies, long- and short-haired, are just a few members of the very large cat family or Felidae, the general name for all felines. These vertebrate mammals, carnivorous, large or small, have common characteristics.

It has taken a very long time to produce the beautiful fur-covered animals we know today. In fact, more than forty million years have passed since their ancestors, the miacids, evolved during the Eocene Period. The miacids were small, catlike creatures, hunters and tree climbers, the forebears of several groups which developed, including those of the bear, the dog, the seal, the civet and the cat families. It is only through fossils, found throughout the world, that we have been able to trace the development of the cat up to the present time and have discovered that the very early cats divided into two groups.

The first was the Hoplophoneus, from which eventually developed the saber-toothed tiger, known to have inhabited America, Asia and Europe. It was a fierce-looking beast, with fangs at least seven inches long, which must have been capable of stabbing its victim to death. The second group was the Dinicitis, which also had large canine teeth, but not as long as those of the saber-toothed tiger. They were tree climbers, able to leap, hunting by stealth, and are said to have been the forebears of all the cats known today.

It may seem strange that the large cats, such as lions and tigers, should be so closely related to the pet cats that are so much a part of our lives, but a visit to any zoo will show convincing common characteristics. At the London Zoological Gardens in Regent's Park, there is a beautiful black female panther, looking like Rudyard Kipling's Bagheera in *The Jungle Book*, with a shining black coat, strong head and big eyes, that, except for her size, could be the twin of many a household pet. The twitching of her tail, the rolling on her back with legs in the air, the low rumbles she gives from time to time, are all mannerisms found in most cats.

The Felidae are preeminently carnivorous in diet, some being carrion eaters, others preferring their meat freshly killed. The body shape is well adapted to the stealthy hunting necessary to catch their prey. Intelligent, swift in movement and silent, with a number being able to climb rocks and trees, they vary in size from the lion, which may weigh up to five hundred pounds, to the little Malayan red cat, weighing only three or four pounds.

The essence of the domestic cat is dealt with in detail in this book, but in the main the Felidae have the same general characteristics: a short, rounded skull connected to the flexible backbone by very strong muscles, enabling the head to be turned swiftly in all directions. The jaw is short, functioning only with an up-and-down movement. The twenty-six baby teeth are shed and replaced by an adult set of thirty. Pointed in shape, they comprise sixteen in the upper jaw and fourteen in the lower, made up of incisors, premolars, molars and the very important canines. Used with a scissorlike action, the teeth enable the cats to grip and tear meat apart rather than chew it, and they are able to swallow chunks of meat with ease.

The tongues are rough, being covered with small hooked papillae that are used to rasp meat off bones, and also to lap, and cleanse the fur.

The cheeks are well developed and the muzzles strong, but short in comparison with those of their early ancestors and the other groups which evolved from them.

The vibrissae, or whiskers, are strong thick hairs, which are extremely sensitive, being connected to nerve centers. They are useful organs of touch, particularly when hunting in half-light, as they enable the animal to feel the way ahead carefully.

The hearing is well developed and most efficient, which

is a necessity for hunting in the wild. The head can be turned rapidly to pick up the slightest sound, with the earflaps acting as parabolas. The way the ears are held is often an indication of the mood of the animal, particularly in the case of the domestic cat.

Most striking are the eyes of some of the Felidae, with the pupils appearing as large round openings in dim light and narrow vertical slits in bright sunshine. In fact, the Chinese are said to have been able to tell the time of the day by the variation in size of their cats' pupils. The eyes in strong light appear as pencil-thin black vertical lines, shutting out the sunshine, while if looked at when it is beginning to get dark, the pupils will be very large to use the small amount of light available. It was once thought that they waxed and waned with the moon. It is untrue to say that cats can see in the dark, but they can certainly see in very dim light, which is essential for night hunters. According to the zoologists, cats are color-blind, seeing only in shades of gray and white, but they appear to have very sharp definition, easily distinguishing a small object from a background of the same color.

It is said frequently that cats have a poor sense of smell. Maybe it is not so highly developed as that of the dog family, but judging by domestic cats which, from a long way off, can certainly smell their food cooking, the sense of smell is more than adequate. Pet cats refuse to eat anything that smells the slightest bit "off," and have to be persuaded to eat at all should they have a cold and be unable to smell the food.

The Felidae are digitigrade, that is, toe walkers, which enables them to move noiselessly when hunting. They

6

have five toes on the front paws and four on the back although, due to a mutation, some domestic cats, known as polydactyls, may have six, even seven, toes on the front and five or six on the back. The paws are padded and the claws are retractile: that is, they can be drawn in and out as required. It was once thought, and frequently said, that the cheetah is an exception, being unable to retract its claws, but it has been proved that it can do so, although it lacks the full skin protection that the other cats' claws have.

Their skeletons, with the flexible backbone and the strong hind legs, coupled with the powerful system of muscles, enable the felines to pounce and spring effortlessly; all their movements are easy and graceful. The tails are thought to be used for balancing and, like the ears, may also indicate moods.

The markings and colorings of the fur vary according to the terrain in which the wild felines live. The tawny coloring of the lion blends into the open country in which it hunts, while the tiger's pattern of markings gives complete camouflage as it hides in the undergrowth for a likely prey. Other felines have spots and bars which make them scarcely discernible in the shadows of the jungles where they live. Through careful breeding, similar markings and colorings are now found in the domestic species.

The litters vary from one to six in number, three being the average, with the period of gestation ranging from 108 days for the lion down to 60 days or thereabouts for the European wildcat.

So much for the general characteristics of the felines, showing that they are all cousins, wild or domestic. Some are very similar in appearance to the domestic cats, but it should be stressed here that anyone thinking of acquiring a small wildcat, such as a margay, as a pet, should think twice about it. Most of these small animals are trapped in the jungle, and often arrive in very poor condition, needing specialized medical attention. It is very cruel to confine these wild felines to cages, accustomed as they are to complete freedom, and frequently they lose condition rapidly and die.

Much has been written about the origins of the first domestic cats, mainly based on supposition, as there is very little concrete evidence to go on, and no one can claim with certainty to know the true history.

These first cats did not happen suddenly but evolved gradually with the possible taming and interbreeding of the smaller desert cats. Several of the wildcats, such as the Caffre and the Indian desert cat, have proved to be tamable. It is possible that their ancestors, as kittens, were brought in by hunters who had killed the parents. They were made much of by the children, were accepted and allowed to stay. Notwithstanding, it must have been many, many years before domestication was achieved, since even when born in captivity, with both parents being comparatively tame, kittens of such cats will not be naturally tame, and some never become so. Obviously, it is from the long-ago ancestors that many traits inherent in the cat of today come. Most cats, as kittens, have a very short relationship with the mother, but hunting and tracking down prey seem to come to most of them by instinct.

Egypt is given the credit for being one of the first countries to have domesticated the cat, possibly the Caffre. There is evidence, pictorial and otherwise, that they were house pets in Egypt more than four thousand years ago.

At first cats were admired only for their prowess in catching snakes, rats and mice. It was in this capacity that they became protectors of the granaries and temples, often cared for by the priests.

Cats gained further respect from their masters for their intelligence and aloofness, and for their skill in hunting fish and fowl, as featured in many wall paintings. Again, from the wall paintings, it would appear that some even acted as retrievers. Later, because of their ability to give birth regularly to numerous kittens, they became symbols of fertility. Plutarch, an early Greek biographer, said that "she [the cat] brings forth at first one kitten, afterwards two, and the third time three; and that number increaseth thus until the seventh and last birth, so that she bears in all twenty-eight young, or as many as the moon hath revolutions." Many ordinary domestic cats have more than a hundred kittens in their lifetimes if allowed to breed unchecked, many having six in their first litters, so Plutarch was very much out in this respect.

The Egyptians worshiped many animals, but probably none more so than the cat, whose excellent qualities they appreciated. In due course, temples were built in honor of the cat, and according to Herodotus, who traveled through Egypt in 450 B.C., the Temple of Bubastis, near Thebes, by the Nile in lower Egypt, was "the fairest in all Egypt." It was here that Pakht, the benign cat-headed goddess with the figure of a woman, was worshiped with much pomp and ceremony. A great festival, which was attended by crowds, sometimes numbering more than seventy thousand from all over Egypt, was held every year at the temple in her honor. This was the beginning of the long history of cat worship which persisted until the end of the ancient Egyptian civilization.

There are numerous figures, statues and murals in existence depicting Pakht, some showing her with a kitten at her feet. In her right hand she holds a sistrum—a phallic symbol—which was a musical instrument, frequently with a small figure of a cat on its top representing fertility, which was carried in processions and shaken like a rattle to repel the evil spirits.

In time, nearly every household had a living cat, often statuettes as well, as protection against evil. And in the event of a fire the first thing to be saved was the cat. Should one be killed, even inadvertently, the killer was punished by death. When a cat died, the whole family went into mourning, shaving off their eyebrows as a token of grief.

In 500 B.C. the cat was still in such an unassailable position that the Persians took advantage of this when fighting to capture Pelusium—now Tisseh—from the Egyptians. The Persian ruler Cambyses collected as many cats as possible and set them loose in front of his soldiers. In addition, each soldier carried a cat before him as a shield. The Egyptians refused to harm their revered cats, and Cambyses won the day.

The Egyptians guarded their sacred cats jealously and their export was forbidden. But, even in those days, smuggling must have been carried on by travelers, as domestic cats began to appear in many other parts of the world. There is no other documentation as thorough as that in Egypt regarding the early domestic cats in other countries, but they were known in India, as mention is made of them in the Sanskrit writings of more than three thousand years ago. It is possible that the development there was much the same as in Egypt, with the taming of the Indian desert cat. India has many legends about them, with the cats being triumphant through stealth and cunning. They were often referred to as "mouse enemies" and "rat eaters," qualities for which cats were much admired.

There is evidence of domestication over two thousand years ago in China, where it was once thought that one became a cat after death. Carl Van Vechten, in *The Tiger in the House,* says that this belief "caused the mighty Empress Wu to forbid cats entrance to her palace, because a lady of the court, before being cruelly put to death, threatened to turn Her Royal Highness into a rat and tease her as a spectre-cat."

They were the subject of adoration by the ladies of China and were appreciated for their rat-catching capabilities. There was a curious, but true, saying that "a lame cat is better than a swift horse when rats infest a palace."

For a while in Japan it was thought necessary only to have an effigy of a cat to keep the mice at bay, but soon it became apparent that a live animal was required. Unhappily, only a few hundred years later, cats came to be regarded as having associations with demons and were feared accordingly. In Tokyo, however, there is a temple where the cats are venerated after death. The little graves are surrounded by statues and paintings of cats and by Buddhist prayer tablets. Featured there are many "good luck" figures of cats with right paws raised, and copies of these are still brought back from Japan by many tourists.

There is no mention of cats by the Hebrews in the Bible, possibly because of their hatred for anything which pertained to Egypt.

Although the Romans gave little early mention to the cat, it is obvious that they took the cult to Italy from Egypt, even eventually building a temple there for the convenience of Egyptian visitors. Cats became a symbol of liberty and were used as emblems on the shields and banners of the Roman legions. They were featured in Roman art, and there is a well-known mosaic in the museum at Naples picturing a cat seizing a bird.

Like most Moslems, the Arabs had a strong liking for cats and were said by Pliny to revere a golden cat. They believed that jinns took the forms of felines and other animals, and that therefore cats were capable of magic powers.

There is the delightful story of the Prophet Mohammed and his cat, Muezza, which fell asleep on the sleeve of his robe, and rather than disturb his pet, the Prophet cut off the sleeve. This little story may account for the high regard in which cats were held in many Eastern countries, including Turkey, where they were allowed the freedom of the mosques.

Greece has little evidence of domestication of early cats, and many authorities suggest that the first "rat catchers" used to protect the granaries were really martens and weasels, not cats. The British Museum has Greek vases depicting creatures said to be cats, but these possibly could be cheetahs. There is a marble relief, discovered in Greece in

1922, which most definitely depicts a cat and a dog being encouraged to fight by two youths, with the animals being held by leads.

It is stated frequently that the Phoenicians, the early traders, were responsible for bringing the domestic cat to Britain. This may be true but cannot be authenticated. The credit is usually given to the Romans, and evidence does point to the fact that until the time of Julius Caesar there were only wildcats in Britain, which were hunted for their skins.

During the excavations of a Roman villa at Lullingstone in Kent, built about A.D. 400, what is thought to be the oldest remains known of a domestic cat were found. Apparently the cat had been killed by a falling beam when the building was burned down. The Romans would have brought their cats with them to protect the granaries against rats and mice, and to have as pets in their villas, but they would have been few in number. There is evidence that even a thousand years after the Roman invasion, cats were still much prized. In A.D. 936, Howell the Good, one of the Princes of Wales, made laws which give the first documentary evidence of the status of the domestic cat and the value placed upon it. The price of a kitten before it could see was one penny, after it caught a mouse, two pennies, and if it gave further proof of its usefulness, four pennies. An order was issued that anyone who stole or killed a cat that guarded the prince's granary was to forfeit a milch ewe, its fleece and lamb, or as much wheat as, when poured on the cat suspended by its tail, with its head touching the floor, would form a heap high enough to cover the tip of the tail. If the cat's qualities were misrepresented, there were severe penalties imposed on the seller, with the purchase price being refunded. Switzerland and Saxony also had similar laws covering the early domestic cats.

Gradually, domestic cats became known in most countries throughout the world, but there is little written history about them until the fifteenth century, when, with the coming of the Inquisition, their popularity suffered an almost total eclipse and they came to be regarded as familiars of the devil and witches. Tales were told of cats sitting behind witches on broomsticks and flying through the air. Harmless old women were tried, found guilty and burned to death with their cats, just because they owned one. Many women were tortured and forced to confess that they were able to change into cats. In a few countries, in those days, to be a twin was almost a death sentence, as it was thought that one of the pair was able to take the form of a cat at will.

The association with witchcraft made the cat the scapegoat for many supposed evils and ill-doings, and torturing one was frequently looked on as a form of entertainment. Any disasters such as crop failures, storms, floods, fires and the like were often thought by the superstitious to be caused by cats, which were put to death by the hundreds. In France bonfires were lit every St. John's Eve for merrymaking and the burning of cats. Hanging, drowning, burning, any horrible way of killing; nothing was too bad for the innocent cats, and this went on for several centuries.

In 1618 the people of Ypres in France were forbidden by statute to practice their usual Lenten custom of throwing cats from the top of the cathedral tower, but it took much longer to stop all the persecution. The eighteenth century saw some enlightenment in the treatment of cats, with France, perhaps, being one of the first countries to return them to favor.

Gradually throughout Europe, they became the pampered pets of the fashionable and wealthy, the companions of artists, writers and poets.

Over the centuries, millions of words have been written about cats, good and bad; indeed, it is difficult to pick out those that are most representative of their periods. M. Oldfield Howey, in *The Cat in the Mysteries of Religion and Magic,* wrote: "The Cat is the symbol of Good and of Evil, of Light and of Darkness, of Christ and of Satan, of Religion and of Black Magic, of Sun and of Moon, of Father, Mother and Son." All very true, as the cat has appeared in many guises, playing many parts.

In legend, it is said that Noah prayed for protection for the stores in the Ark from the ravages of mice. In answer to his prayer, the lion sneezed, and from his nostrils came the first pair of cats. The sight of them so frightened the mice that they vanished into their nearest holes, which have been their hiding places from that day.

Another legend has it that the cat was so anxious to leave the Ark when the floods had subsided that she jumped up to get out of the window quickly. As she did so, the dog snapped at her, biting off her tail, which resulted in the first Manx cats, and is also the reason for the enmity between dogs and cats ever since.

In Scandinavia, Freya, the goddess of love and beauty, identified with Venus, the goddess of love, rode in a chariot drawn by two domestic cats. Freya was also identified with Nerthus, her mother, the symbol of all-supporting earth, and those who placed milk in the cornfields for her cats were said to be given special protection for their crops in bad weather.

In Greek mythology, there is mention of Diana, the moon goddess, who is said to have created the cat as retaliation and to ridicule her brother, Apollo, who had created the lion, the king of the beasts, to frighten her.

Many storybooks have been written about cats. One of the first about their history and beginnings was the *Book of Cats* by Charles H. Ross, which was written in 1867 and required considerable research. One chapter is headed "Of Pussy Poorly and some curiosities of the Cats' meat trade." The author tells of a cats' meat seller making as much as £1000 at the business; this would probably be the sum total, as the meat sold at 2½d per pound, a price which would make the breeders of today very envious. Charles Ross's book was well received and proved to be the forerunner of many such books by many different authors. It is incredible to think that the year in which it appeared also saw a trial for witchcraft, involving a cat, in the New World.

A small handbook, *The Domestic Cat,* written by Gordon Stables in 1876, must have been exceedingly useful to cat lovers, dealing as it did with the varieties known at that time.

It should be remembered that these books appeared at a time when interest was beginning to be focused on "fancy" cats, and that in 1871 Harrison Weir had organized the first official cat show at the Crystal Palace and had drawn up points of excellence for their judging. Eventually he produced a book, *Our Cats and All About Them,* which he said was the "outcome of over fifty years' careful, thoughtful, heedful observation, much research, and not unprofitable attention to the facts and fancies of others." This book is treasured nowadays, forming as it did the foundation for the whole Cat Fancy throughout the world, by giving details of the first varieties of pedigreed cats, with their standards.

In 1903, Miss Frances Simpson, a cat judge and breeder, produced one of the most comprehensive books on cats ever written, *The Book of the Cat.* She wrote knowledgeably on all the varieties, and is quoted as an authority by many authors. The hundreds of charming illustrations are a valuable guide to the types and markings of the early cats whose names appear on pedigrees as the ancestors of many famous modern cats.

Events in Europe leading up to the 1914–18 war saw a lessening of interest for a while in the breeding of and writing on pedigreed cats, but one book published soon after the war proved a ready seller. This was *The Tiger in the House,* by Carl Van Vechten, outstanding in its day for information on cats in folklore, art, music, the theater and fiction among much else. From his writing, he was a man who must have loved and understood cats. Of the cat he wrote: "He gives his affection where it pleases him to give it (when, also, it might be added) and he withholds it from those whom he deems unworthy of it. In other words with a cat you stand on much the same footing that you stand with a fine and dignified friend; if you forfeit his respect and confidence the relationship suffers."

Apart from practical books, so much has been written about cats, as I found when doing research for this book, that it is quite bewildering. There are fairy tales, legends, stories, plays, articles and poems, some well known, others not.

One of the earliest was a fable by Aesop, the Greek slave, who, according to legend, lived about 620–560 B.C. He could not have been a cat lover, as the fable "The Cat, the Eagle and the Sow" shows the cat in a very poor light, making mischief between her two neighbors, who shared a tree with her, the moral given being "Beware of mischief makers."

In the fourteenth century, Chaucer mentioned cats in his *Canterbury Tales* more than once, saying:

> *Lat take a cat and fostre him wel with milke,*
> *And tendre flesh, and make his couche of silk.*

Shakespeare made over forty references to cats, none being particularly complimentary. It should be remembered that during his lifetime the cat was beginning to fall into disrepute and was becoming associated with witchcraft. He had this in mind probably when one of the witches in *Macbeth* says, "Thrice the brindled cat hath mew'd." Shylock, in *The Merchant of Venice,* speaks of the "harmless necessary cat," which was mild for Shakespeare, as Romeo speaks of "Every cat and dog, and little mouse, every unworthy thing," while another of Shakespeare's characters, Cornelius, says, "Creatures vile, as cats and dogs, of no esteem."

Ben Jonson is credited with saying, " 'Tis a pity you had not ten lives—a cat's and your own." The figure "nine" is used frequently in connection with cats, with many references to their nine lives. The cat in John Gay's fable, "The Old Woman and Her Cats," says:

> *'Tis infamy to serve a hag*
> *Cats are thought imps, her broom a nag;*
> *And boys against our lives combine,*
> *Because, 'tis said, your cats have nine.*

James Boswell, the biographer and an ailurophobe, wrote of Dr. Johnson's cat, Hodge, and the attention his master showed him by personally buying him oysters, rather than trouble the servants.

The affection Abraham Lincoln had for cats is well known. In the Civil War, when visiting General Grant, the president noticed three tiny, motherless kittens in the tent and asked that they be well cared for, inquiring after them daily. Lincoln's biographer, William Herndon, says that "when . . . weariness set in he would stop thought and get down and play with a little dog or kitten to recover." Time and time again, many famous men have found pleasure and relaxation in playing with their cats. Indeed, Sir Winston Churchill's was such a pet that he allowed it to sleep on the bed, and had a chair set at the table for him.

Although not professing to be a cat lover, Charles Dickens mentioned them frequently in his books and owned one called Willamina, who insisted on her kittens being in his study. They were removed several times, but she brought them back, until at last he gave in and allowed them to stay.

Edgar Allan Poe's "The Black Cat" is not really a cat for

cat lovers, but, in fact, in Poe's short, often unhappy life, his beloved cat Caterina was a much-cherished companion.

Mark Twain owned a number of cats, calling them such names as Blatherstike and Zoroaster, to teach his children how to pronounce difficult words. There are a number of references to cats in his writings, showing his fondness for them.

More recently, we have Rudyard Kipling and "The Cat That Walked by Himself," and writers such as Michael Joseph and his popular book on his Siamese, *Charles, the story of a Friendship;* Paul Gallico's charming book, *Jennie;* and Pamela and James Mason's *The Cats in Our Lives.* Compton Mackenzie, Beverley Nichols, Doreen Tovey and Derek Tangye all show their deep affection for cats in their various writings.

Children's fondness for cats and kittens has always been realized, and many will agree with M. Champfleury, the French author, who said: "The cat is the nurse's favourite and the baby's earliest friend."

We are conditioned to like cats almost from babyhood, being taught to recite "Pussy cat, pussy cat, where have you been?" "Hey diddle diddle, / the cat and the fiddle," "I love little pussy, / her coat is so warm," "Three little kittens they lost their mittens!" and all about the cat that killed the rat in "The House That Jack Built."

Every worthwhile nursery-tale book tells of Dick Whittington and his cat, who together trudged to London to find that the streets were not made of gold. At Highgate Hill, London, there is a small stone and a statue commemorating the fact that the sound of the bells he heard there and the encouragement of his cat made him decide to stay. Eventually, he found fame and fortune.

Puss-in-Boots also tells of a cat that brought fame and fortune to his owner, although this was accomplished by stealth and subterfuge.

Lewis Carroll's Cheshire cat in *Alice's Adventures in Wonderland* is known to most children, and *Through the Looking Glass* starts with the delightful description of Dinah the cat washing her kittens' faces. "First she held the poor thing down by its ear with one paw . . ." Beatrix Potter's books still captivate children. All are concerned with animals, and many mention cats, such as *The Story of Miss Moppet* and *The Tale of Tom Kitten.* Kathleen Hale's "Orlando" has had many strange adventures since he first appeared in 1938, often also involving his wife, Grace, and his kittens.

Many poets have had a deep understanding of cats, making them their close companions and the subject of poems. Robert Herrick wrote:

> *A cat I keep*
> *that plays about my house*
> *Grown fat with eating*
> *Many a miching mouse.*

And William Cowper said of his cat:

> *A poet's cat, sedate and grave*
> *As poet well could wish to have.*

One of the best known of Edward Lear's nonsense songs is "The Owl and the Pussy-cat," who "went to sea in a beautiful pea-green boat," but it is not always realized how devoted he was to his cat, Foss, his constant companion. Foss lived to be seventeen, with Lear dying a few months afterwards.

W. B. Yeats wrote a poem to "The Cat and The Moon" about Minnaloushe who

> *lifts to the changing moon His changing eyes,*

and William Wordsworth wrote, while watching a kitten playing with falling leaves, "How she starts, crouches, stretches, paws and darts." But Swinburne's cat was most sedate when the poet wrote: "Stately, kindly, lordly friend condescend here to sit by me."

"To fight like Kilkenny cats" is a well-known saying, but perhaps the Irish poem itself is lesser known. In several verses it tells how they fought:

> *Till, excepting their nails*
> *and the tips of their tails,*
> *Instead of two cats,*
> *there wasn't any.*

Another, lesser-known work, now found only occasionally in secondhand bookshops, is the charming *Rubaiyat of a Persian Kitten*, written in 1904 by Oliver Herford. One verse says:

> *Myself when young did eagerly frequent*
> *The backyard fence and heard Great Argument*
> *About it, and about, yet evermore*
> *Came out with fewer fur than in I went.*

T. S. Eliot's *Old Possum's Book of Practical Cats* is world famous, not only for the rhymes but also for the splendid names of his "men about town" cats. Who could forget Mungojerrie and Rumpelteaser, "a notorious couple of cats," or Rum Tum Tugger, "a curious cat."

Cats have been featured in art over the centuries in various ways and forms since they first appeared in Egyptian murals. Paintings and cartoons by famous artists, films, advertisements and commercials on television portray different facets of these creatures of fascinating change and contradiction.

It is difficult to draw or paint cats satisfactorily. They are so swift in movement and such bundles of energy that they will rarely sit still long enough to be models. This is probably one of the reasons there are so many pictures of sleeping cats.

Italian, Dutch and Flemish schools of painting have shown cats in a number of sacred pictures. Jan Brueghel painted Adam and Eve being driven out of Eden, with the cat stretched out, fast asleep, typically ignoring the whole proceedings. Leonardo da Vinci's drawings captured the cat in typical poses.

Dürer, Jan Fyt, Rembrandt, Manet, Hogarth, Tintoretto and Picasso are just a few of the artists who have depicted cats in many moods, some as homely pets, others aristocratic, some really horrific, and yet others as mere shadows in the background.

Gottfried Mind, the Swiss artist, was famous for his bear and cat paintings. That he loved cats comes out very clearly, and when rabies broke out in Berne and most of the cats were killed, he was heartbroken, although he did manage to save his constant companion, Minette.

The Japanese have shown great feeling for cats in many of their paintings. Utamaro in the eighteenth century and Kuniyoshi in the twentieth century both drew delightful cat studies, and the latter's caricatures of actors as cats are still very amusing.

Henriette Ronner, the Dutch artist, enjoyed a considerable vogue in the late nineteenth and early twentieth centuries, with her numerous portraits of cats, many of which were bought by royalty. Seen today, the cats and kittens she depicted, mostly long-haired, are sweet, but "chocolate box" in appearance and lacking in character.

In the cat world, one of the best-known names for cat pictures and sketches was that of Louis Wain, onetime president of the National Cat Club (Great Britain) and an international cat judge. Drawn chiefly for children, but mostly appreciated by adults, his humorous cat pictures give a remarkable insight into life in Britain at the turn of the century, showing cats living and playing as humans in all walks of life. For many years, calendars, Christmas cards and children's annuals illustrated by him appeared regularly, until he met with a serious road accident. After this he became mentally ill and was confined to a mental home for many years until he died in 1939. During this period his cat drawings became more and more eccentric, showing very clearly the deterioration of his mind.

Reading about the artists, one realizes that those having deep affection for cats seemed able to picture them most realistically, catching them in characteristic poses, often succeeding in showing their personalities, while artists who used them purely as models never made them look anything but wooden.

Apart from paintings, cats have appeared in heraldry

through the ages, in inn signs, in wood carvings frequently found in churches and in trademarks of all descriptions. From the bronze statuettes of the early Egyptians and the clay images found in South America, models of cats, whether in wood, china, glass, metal or even gold, have always been popular.

For many years cats have appeared in the press throughout of the world, advertising merchandise ranging from cigarettes to carpets, and have even made their appearance on a series of postage stamps.

Since "Felix the Cat" took his first walk across the silver screen, cats have appeared in many cartoons and films. Walt Disney featured them in several full-length films, where they succeeded in stealing the thunder from the stars.

On television, one of the most famous cats in Britain, a Siamese called Jason, appeared regularly in a children's program, receiving his own fan mail and attracting children in the hundreds when he made personal appearances. His place has now been taken by two short-haired British cats, a Silver Spotted and a Silver Tabby. A white cat, Arthur, won fame and publicity in a commercial on television for a certain cat food by always eating it with his paw. His place has now been taken by another short-haired white, Sam, who also uses his paw to eat his food. Thanks to television, cats have been brought even more into the public eye as they have been used for advertising many things, and in some cases they have become so valuable that, when appearing at cat shows, they have to be guarded by security officers and insured for a considerable sum of money, sometimes in excess of $2,000.

So much for the general history of the domestic cat. As

far as one can tell they were originally short-haired, but, by the end of the sixteenth century, possibly earlier, cats with long fur began to appear in Europe. Nicholas Claude Fabri de Peirese, a naturalist and scientist, is credited with bringing the first Angora to France, presumably from Turkey. Since it is known that the fur can change through a mutation and that the Rex cats with their curly coats arose by chance in the first place, it is possible that the long coat also started through a mutation. It is probable that a cat with thick fur living in a confined district, such as a mountainous area, had a litter with longer fur than usual, and interbreeding set the coat length. The fur of the early long-hairs was not as luxurious as that seen today, which has resulted from years of planned breeding for coat length.

At first, the cats with long fur were referred to as Asiatic or Eastern cats to distinguish them from the short-haired European or Western cats. They were thought to have originated in Angora—now Ankara—in Turkey. They were said to have been in all shades, with white cats being the most sought after, particularly if their hearing was good. It has been known for years that deafness is inherent in certain strains of white cats with blue eyes. The early Angoras had small heads, long noses, tall ears and clinging silky coats, very similar to the type of Turkish cat recognized today.

Long-hairs from Persia followed, but they do not seem to exist as natives in that country today. In fact, many are exported to Persia from Britain. These original Persians had ruffs around the head, broader heads, smaller ears and bigger eyes than those of the Angoras. The coats were longer, fuller and less silky, with the colors being varied but black being much sought after.

In the elegant drawing rooms in Paris, the cats from Angora were made much of. They were given silken cushions to sleep on, were bedecked with ribbons and were considered very ornamental. In due course, they were exported to England, where they were known for a time as French cats.

In Europe, as the number of cats with long coats increased, the popularity of those with short fur suffered, and it remained that way until the Siamese appeared on the scene, rapidly becoming the most popular pedigreed cat. Today, the long-hairs are once again increasing in popularity.

In America, the first domesticated cats arrived with the Pilgrim Fathers and early missionaries. Over the years, the settlers arrived with their cats, and the numbers increased gradually. In 1749, cats were imported to Pennsylvania to combat the rats, while in 1750 in Paraguay, a pound of gold was paid for one domestic cat. Figures of animals that could be cats were made by the Incas in Peru long ago, but it is not known if they were models of domestic cats.

In the 1850s, cats with longish fur began to be seen in Maine. Sailors brought them back from Turkey on the Yankee clippers, and these cats interbred with local short-haired domestic cats. The results were strong, sturdy cats of Angora type, with thick coats, often with tabby markings, which became known as the Maine Coon cats. In many cases, the fur resembled that of the raccoon, and before it was appreciated that it was biologically impossible, the cats were thought to be part raccoon. By the end of the nineteenth century, many prizewinning cats made their way to the United States from Britain. Cat shows started, breeding began in earnest and today the Cat Fancy and interest in pedigreed-cat breeding are increasing, as indeed they are in Britain and in many other countries in the world, all in the short period of one hundred years or thereabouts.

There are many books which give full details of the varieties recognized, but people frequently want to know which variety makes the best pet. The best pet ultimately, whatever the variety, usually belongs to the owner with the most common sense, who does not fuss unduly, but has time to give the cat the attention it requires. If a kitten is treated badly and pulled about by young children, it may well grow up to be spiteful and bad tempered, while one that is almost ignored by the owner and given very little affection may become a bored, lethargic cat.

It is as well, too, to consider the advantages and disadvantages of owning a cat.

The Advantages

Cats need not be taken out for exercise, although some will walk on leads if trained to do so when young.

Being small animals, they will live happily in an apartment or house, provided they are encouraged to play and time is allowed for this.

All feeding is expensive these days, but cats are not large eaters and do well on raw or cooked meat, commercial cat food and some extras to make for variety. Fish may be given, but a cat fed exclusively on fish may develop skin trouble. Milk is not essential, but water should always be available.

If neutered, cats are rarely noisy, although unaltered males and females can be, particularly when the latter are in season.

If necessary, cats can travel in carriers and accompany their owners. In Britain, they can be taken out of the country only if, on their return, the owner is prepared to pay for the cat to go into quarantine for six months, with compulsory rabies injections being given during that period. No one may bring any cat into Britain unless it goes into quarantine with the necessary permits being obtained well in advance.

Cats make constant companions for many years.

The Disadvantages

A cat can live a very long time, fifteen to eighteen years being quite usual, and will always be a responsibility for the owner, in that it will need daily attention, particularly when holidays come around.

The feeding, preparing, cooking and washing up, even the buying and the cost of the food, can be a nuisance.

If there is no garden, litter boxes are essential and will need constant changing, as cats are very fussy.

Time will be needed for grooming, although this will vary considerably with the variety, the long-hairs requiring the most attention.

The Choice

There are three main groups, long-hairs, short-hairs, (British and Foreign) and the Siamese, so the choice is large.

The long-hairs, often referred to as Persians, are popular. They are very aristocratic in appearance, having large round eyes, short noses, small ears and long silky fur, and are most photogenic whether asleep or awake. To many, their decorative appearance cannot be faulted.

In character and behavior they are considered much quieter than the Siamese, but they can be very talkative, almost to the extent of holding a conversation, invariably answering when spoken to. Individual in character, they are quite happy to be the only cat in a household—many preferring it. They show affection readily and love being fussed over. As in all varieties, the intelligence varies considerably, and some are very bright, soon learning simple tricks. They love to be noticed and are very playful and lively, even when old.

The varieties of Persians include the self-colors, that is, the same color all over. These are the Blacks; the Whites, which may have orange eyes, blue eyes or an eye of each color; the Red Selfs; the Creams; and most popular of all, the Blues. There are Tabbies: the Silvers with contrasting black markings, and the Reds with markings a deeper color than that of the main coat. The Chinchillas are also a very popular variety, with their long, flowing white coats delicately tipped with black; their eyes, unlike the majority of the long-hairs, are emerald or blue-green in color. Unrecognized in Britain, but known in some other countries, are the Shaded Silvers, which have definite shadings rather than tippings of black on the white undercoat. There are two varieties of Smokes—the Blacks and the Blues; and although they are one of the oldest known in the Cat Fancy, they are still comparatively rare, and a kitten may have to be ordered well in advance. Referred to frequently as the cat of contrasts, the Black Smokes are most striking, with almost white undercoats and black top coats. From a distance, the cat may look black, and it is not until it moves that the gleaming white undercoat may be seen. In Blue Smokes, the blue replaces the black.

The Tortoiseshells and the Tortoiseshell and Whites are most attractive. The former's coat should be broken into patches of black, red and cream, while the Tortie and White has the addition of white. These two are female-only varieties, any male born invariably being sterile. The Blue-Creams, another female-only variety, should have the blue and cream fur softly intermingled, giving the appearance of shot silk, for the British standard, but the American standard calls for the coats to be blue with cream patches. Bicolors have coats of two colors; any solid color and white is allowed, with the black and white and the red and white being very distinctive.

The very striking Himalayan has a coat pattern as found in the Siamese; that is, the points (the face, ears, legs and tail) are a darker color than the pale, creamish body. The points may be seal, brown-blue, chocolate, lilac, red or tortie. All Himalayans should have bright blue eyes.

In the United States, Cameos are recognized. These are similar to the Chinchillas, with red tipping rather than black. There is also a Shaded Cameo with red shading, a Smoke Cameo with red contrasts and a Tabby Cameo.

All the long-hairs mentioned should have much the same type and characteristics, with broad round heads, small ears, frills around the head, big round eyes, stocky bodies on short legs and short full tails.

Other varieties that are included in the long-haired are the Birman and the Turkish. They differ in type in that the heads are not so round, the fur not so luxurious and the tails not so short. The Birmans have a very distinctive feature in that the paws are white, like little gloves on the front legs and with the white going up to a point on the back legs. The body colorings are pale, and like the Himalayans, they have contrasting points and bright blue eyes.

As mentioned before, the Turkish are similar in type to the original Angoras, the heads being short-wedged in shape, with large ears, the bodies long and the full tails medium in length. The fur is chalk white, with auburn markings on the face and auburn rings on the tail.

It is also possible to produce long-hairs through selective or crossbreeding. These may be any coloring, as they have no recognized standard. All varieties need daily brushing and combing if the fur is not to mat up or the cat to get fur ball.

As may be seen, the choice in the long-hairs is very much a matter of taste. All the kittens are charming and entertaining, small, fluffy bundles of energy, on short legs, with little short tails held stiffly in the air. If brought up correctly, they are in no way delicate, nor is special heating required. They are mischievous, playful and lovable. To some, the short noses and big eyes seem to give the long-hairs a bad-tempered look, but they are not at all aggressive in temperament, mostly being gentle by nature.

The British short-hair has a reputation for having an equable temperament and imperturbable nature. Square and sturdy on powerful legs, it has a round, broad head, full cheeks, a shortish nose, small rounded ears, big round eyes and a shortish tail. The fur is short and thick, and must never be too fluffy. The short fur makes grooming comparatively easy with a daily light brushing and combing to keep the coat in good order.

The colors and coat patterns are much the same as those of the long-hairs, ranging from the White down to the Smoke, with the British Blue being the most popular. It is also possible to have Spotties, with distinct spotted markings all over the body, and no stripes are allowed except on the head.

In the United States, there are the American short-hairs, descended from the original domestic cats seen there. The heads are not so round as those of the Britishers. There are also the Exotic short-hairs, which are almost long-hair type with a medium-length coat. Both these varieties come in colors similar to those of the long-hairs.

One variety that differs from all others is the Manx; it has no tail at all and an indentation where the tail should start. It is also possible to have a Stumpie, which has a stump of a tail. The Manx has a double coat, with a thick undercoat and slightly longer outer coat. Almost any color is allowed. The Manx stands higher on the back legs, with the long hindquarters giving the cat a rabbitlike walk.

The idea of having a pet that is unique seems to appeal to people. A would-be owner considering breeding Manx would do well to talk to those already breeding them. It has been found that breeding Manx to Manx may produce a lethal factor, with the kittens dying soon after birth. Cats with tails may produce Manx if mated correctly, so it is important to study the pedigrees well. Weaning may be a little more difficult than for other varieties, with the milk intake having to be carefully monitored.

There are a number of varieties referred to collectively as

Foreign short-hairs, although they are not identical in type. The word "Foreign" should not be taken to mean that the cats come from abroad, although in some instances, way back, similar cats may have originated in particular countries, but today they are usually the results of selective breeding over many years.

The Siamese, with their striking coloring and coat pattern, have long been the most popular of the short-haired varieties. Foreign in type, medium in size, their bodies are long and slender on fine slim legs with small oval paws, and with long, tapering tails. Their heads should be long with good width between the eyes, narrowing to fine muzzles, making a wedge shape. The large pricked ears should be wide at the base, and the almond-shaped eyes a clear, brilliant, deep blue.

The body coloring varies according to the points, being cream in the Seal, glacial white in the Blue, ivory in the Chocolate, and in keeping with the Lilac, the Red, the Tabby, the Tortie, the Cream-Pointed and the other dilutions which are possible. The last five mentioned are known in the United States as Colorpoint short-hairs, not Siamese.

Restless by nature, the Siamese like companionship and the opportunity to be always "doing" things. They take readily to leads and to travel, liking to go everywhere with their owners. Although they are said by many to be one-man cats, a great deal depends on their upbringing, as many Siamese live happily with families with many children.

They are not always noisy, although their cry does differ from that of other cats, and a calling female can sometimes beat any banshee with her wailing! Unlike some varieties, they usually welcome the companionship of another Siamese, particularly if their owners are out most of the day. They are highly intelligent individuals, being very definite in their likes and dislikes.

Early training is essential, as the kittens can be very agile and, if allowed to do so unheeded, will readily climb up curtains and furniture, possibly doing some damage.

The kittens are born white, with the points gradually appearing as the kittens grow, usually during the second or third week. Lively, inquisitive, they are very forward for their ages compared with some varieties, and if not watched will soon clamber out of their boxes and be away.

In the United States, there is also the Balinese with Siamese type and colorings, but the coat is longish, fine and silky. Another variety is the Bombay, not known by that name in Britain, with fine short black fur, a round head, medium-sized ears, medium body and a straight, medium-length tail. Both these varieties are said to make most attractive and amicable pets. There is also the Japanese Bobtail, a very distinctive variety, the tail being only about three inches long, with the fur growing on it being slightly longer and thicker than the body hair, giving a pom-pom effect. The medium-length, soft, silky fur may be white, black, red, black and white, red and white, or the traditional mi-kee coloring of black, red and white. The head shape is almost that of a triangle, while the set of the eyes is such that the cat has a definite Japanese look. Introduced into the United States comparatively recently, they are as yet unknown in Britain.

The Maine Coon cat previously referred to is a muscular, sturdy cat with a heavy, shaggy coat, which may be practically any color. The head is medium in width and in length, with large, wide-set eyes. The tail is long and tapering, covered with long, flowing fur.

For generations the Maine Coon cats have been much sought after as pets. They are very affectionate, and although sometimes they may have an aloof look, this is far from the case as regards their characters, as most are very friendly, love attention and like to be noticed.

The Russian Blues have definite Foreign type, the heads being distinguished by flat and narrow skulls with receding foreheads and green, almond-shaped eyes. The ears are large and pointed, wide at the base, with very little fur to cover them. The short, close-lying coats have a beautiful sheen, the tails are long and tapering and the legs long and slender on dainty, oval paws.

Very quiet in character, they will live happily in apartments, being particularly attached to their owners, but not always clamoring for attention. Although agile by nature, they are not given to climbing about indoors or scratching the furniture. They are usually good with children. Like most of the Foreign varieties, they will exercise on leads and readily take to car travel.

The Abyssinians are unusual in having strikingly ticked coats, with each hair in the fur having two or three bands of darker color. The original Abyssinians have ruddy-brown fur, and there are also the Reds, with rich copper-red fur, the Blues, the Creams and other colorings, but all must have the darker banding. The heads are long, but not so wedge-shaped as the Siamese; the bodies are slender and the tails fairly long and tapering. White markings are faults, but white chins, although undesirable, are allowed.

The Abyssinians have great charm, making ideal companions, loving company, being almost too friendly sometimes. They dislike being kept in confined spaces, pacing up and down like lions. They can be readily trained to a lead, and usually appreciate car travel.

The Havanas, known in the United States as Oriental Chestnuts, are much the same type as the Siamese, with long heads, large pricked ears, graceful, lithe bodies on dainty legs and long, whiplike tails. The Oriental-shaped eyes are green in color. Pink pads on the paws are distinctive. Very gentle, intelligent cats, they are very playful but quiet in character, making ideal pets.

Foreign Whites, Foreign Lilacs and the Oriental shorthairs, which come in a variety of colors, have similar build and type to that of the Havanas. The fur should be short, fine and glossy.

The Burmese, introduced into Britain from the United States in the 1940s, have made such rapid strides in numbers, colors and popularity that they are now nearly as popular as the Siamese. The heads should be short wedges, with slight rounding at the top. The bodies are long and dainty on slim legs, with small oval feet. The tails are long and tapering but should not be too whiplike. The almond-shaped eyes should be chartreuse in color, and the close-lying coats short and glossy. Although only the Brown is recognized in the United States, in Britain it is possible to choose from many colors, ranging from the original Brown with rich, dark, seal-brown fur, to the Blue with coat of bluish-gray, the Chocolate, the Lilac, the Red, the Brown Tortie, the Cream and the Chocolate and Lilac Torties, all having similar build and differing only in coat coloring.

The Burmese are real personalities, affectionate and intelligent. They take readily to leads and traveling in cars, liking to accompany their owners everywhere. They need comparatively little grooming of their short, shining coats, but they like hard stroking with the hands, which will accentuate the shine.

The Korats are short-hairs with close-lying coats solid slate in color, with a silvery sheen. Foreign in type, they have small heads with heart-shaped faces and large ears. The bodies are medium in size, well-muscled, and the tails medium in length. They are affectionate cats and like attention. Hard hand stroking makes their coats shine.

The Devon and Cornish Rex are included with the Foreign varieties, although their short coats differ from other cats, in being curly and wavy, and having no guard hairs. Originally a cat was discovered in Cornwall with a curly coat and it was realized that it was a new mutation. Mating back to the mother produced more Rex-coated kittens, and it was found possible to breed this variety to order. Later, a cat with a similar coat was found in Devon, and it was hoped that the two varieties could interbreed, but this was not so, and both varieties were therefore recognized, being called after the counties in which they were found.

The Cornish coats should be short, thick and plushy, without guard hairs, while the heads should be medium wedge in shape, with flat skulls and straight noses, with large ears and oval-shaped eyes. The medium-slender bodies should be hard and muscular on long straight legs, and the tails long, fine and tapering. The Devon cats are similar, but the noses should have a strongly marked stop, with the muzzles short with a whisker break. The ears, too, are set differently on the wedge-shaped heads. The Devon coats should be very short and fine, wavy and soft, without guard hairs. All coat colors are permitted, but white markings (except in Tortie and Whites) are faults in the Devon, although if symmetrical they are allowed in the Cornish.

The Rex are among the easiest cats to groom, with hard hand stroking being sufficient to keep the coats looking soft and shining. They have pleasing personalities, are very friendly and affectionate and must be one of the family if they are to be happy. They have quiet natures, but are very playful and like to be noticed.

These, then, are, just briefly, details of the various types and colors and so on found in the world of pedigreed cats today. Invariably over the years, other colors and coat patterns will be produced, but the independent character and lovable personality of the individual cat will remain, with the one that you own always being the best one on earth.

The Intelligent Cat

Intelligence is a most difficult characteristic to define, but it would seem to denote a comprehension of situations and the ability to select from patterns of behavior offered. That the cat has high intelligence is obvious to anyone who has ever lived with one of these creatures, and curiosity, so obviously present in every cat, is a mark of intelligence in any animal.

Cats are far less influenced by the basic drives of hunger, thirst and fear than are many other animals, and this is why they are difficult to train in performing tricks, so readily undertaken by dogs for small rewards—a sugar lump or biscuit, for example. A reward for the cat needs to be much more than a mere morsel of food. Most cats would rather starve to death than eat if they are unhappy in a strange environment, such as a new home or a boarding cattery. It is difficult to know for sure whether the cat would really go this far, rather than give in, but it is common for such animals to need veterinary forced feeding to get them back to health.

Intelligence tests have been used by animal behaviorists on many animals, and the cat has been found to be difficult to get to collaborate, being little influenced by the action/reward processes used in such tests. Usually, cats are employed in laboratories for experimentation on areas of the brain where electrodes are inserted into individual neurons and neuronal activity recorded electrically.

Stories of cats returning to their old homes over miles of unfamiliar, previously unseen terrain are fascinating and point to a high degree of intelligence. The direction of travel is possibly instinctive, but intelligence may be deduced when one considers the effort that must be made to survive such journeys—finding food in unfamiliar areas, seeking sheltered resting places and avoiding notice from humans, with, above all, the determination to keep going until the goal is reached.

Cats learn to open window latches and to swing on door handles with just the right angle of leverage to cause the door to swing open. They learn to pry open the door of the refrigerator, and know just when the burner of the stove is cool enough to sit on without getting burned. They know exactly what time the master or mistress is due home, and many cats get up and stretch, then go to the door to wait, right at the appointed time, but on Sundays, they do not even bother to wake up! Their patience is infinite, as anyone who has tried to watch a cat watching a mouse hole will confirm, and they are masters of concealment as you will know if you have ever tried to find a cat in the garden when it has decided it is too early to come indoors.

How do cats know that you are about to go on holiday before you even get the suitcases out of the attic? Every boarding cattery owner gets frantic phone calls each year— "We just cannot find Timmy anywhere, he seems to have disappeared!" They also know when you are about to take them to the veterinarian before you even get the cat carrier out.

House cats learn to live in harmony with their people, who appreciate and love the cat's high level of intelligence. Most cats, not allowed to climb all over the dining table or work surfaces in the kitchen, do so only when their people are out of the room. In fact, no one ever sees a cat stealing the cream, the butter, the cheese or the gravy; the cat is in its basket when you go out of the room and still there when you return, but the goodies have mysteriously disappeared and there are sweaty little paw prints on the Formica tops!

Some cats are so fastidious in their habits that they learn to use the toilet. In one family, the youngest child was chastised for not flushing the toilet and for not using any toilet paper, although he protested his innocence loudly. Eventually, the family Siamese neuter was seen, balanced on the edge of the seat one morning, a look of intense concentration on his face. Whenever the door was left off the latch, he would use the toilet instead of his litter box.

Other cats, if used to going out for their toilet, will use the waste drain of a handy sink if left shut indoors for too long a period. This intelligent thinking proves that the cat has worked out that this is the nearest to outside that it can get! One cat hated to make a mess indoors and would wait for hours rather than use the tray left for the purpose. When he eventually had to go, he would sit muttering loud curses, then leap from the tray and run at breakneck speed to the very farthest point in the house, still murmuring darkly.

Cats have been known to set traps for birds by taking scraps of food and setting them down near a place of concealment for themselves. Hiding in wait, the cat pounces out, catching the birds which come down to the bait. Cats also wait patiently for animals such as squirrels when they know they regularly visit a corn store or barn for food. And the patience of the cat, lying practically motionless, only the very tip of the tail twitching with anticipation, the eyes narrowed to fine slits, makes it the ideal vermin catcher on any farm.

Experiments with cats in gadgets known as puzzle boxes have proved this species' high intelligence. Whereas the normal tests used on dogs, monkeys and rats use the food or pleasure reward system for testing performance, the puzzle boxes were designed with varying degrees of difficulty in opening the doors from the inside. Cats were put inside the boxes and left to see if they could work out how to get out. Even quite complicated hook-and-hasp catches were quickly manipulated by the cats, effecting their escape. If a cat was replaced in a box from which it had taken some time to learn how to escape, it was amazing to notice how quickly it was able to use its previously learned experience in order to escape much more speedily.

Dog lovers often make derogatory remarks about the cat's lack of intelligence, supporting their views by remarking that cats are difficult to train, will not come when called and do not perform tricks. Is it a mark of intelligence to perform tricks? Is it a lack of intelligence to ignore a command to attend one's master? Or is it just that the cat is independent and prefers to do exactly what it wants, when it wants to?

The Evolution
of the Cat's Brain

In order to understand better the function and complexity of the cat's brain and nervous system, it is necessary to learn a little of its evolution. We need not, however, concern ourselves with details of evolutionary theories but merely need to know that the basic assumptions are that variations among living organisms occur regularly, and that some prove to be more adaptive than others. The organism with the adaptive variation has a competitive advantage in its environment and is, therefore, more likely to survive and reproduce itself than its less fortunate relatives. In the cat family, it is adaptation that has caused the jungle-dwelling tiger to have its outline-disguising stripes, while the plains lion is the color of the fine dust it treads. Small cats are naturally tabby—spotted, barred or striped—the dappled pattern breaking their outlines, thus allowing them to remain concealed from both predators and prey.

Another important feature in the evolution of the domestic cat, and the reason it has remained virtually unaltered for so long, would appear to be the highly specialized dentition. The well-designed jaws are equipped with a range of teeth to cope with grasping prey, holding it and tearing the flesh.

As variations are transmitted by heredity, so evolution continues, and successful variations survive to reproduce while unsuccessful ones die out. In the far-distant past, organisms would perhaps move to new environments and have to adapt to changes in food, climate or altitude; hence the great diversity of species found in the world today. As this book is concerned with the behavior of the cat, we must also learn something about the evolution of its brain and nervous system, for being a solitary animal, it relies upon the efficiency of its own central nervous system for survival in the wild. This system has evolved to a design which makes the species among the most alert, perceptive and coordinated of all mammals.

In the beginning, there were one-celled animals which had no nervous system, although chemical reactions in the single cell enabled the organism to move about, to engulf food, but to avoid toxic substances. The sponge, a multicelled animal, has cells which conduct impulses individually, but still has no trace of a nervous system. Once we reach animals such as the polyps, however, the first signs of organized nerve cells are found. These cells, or neurons, are spread evenly throughout the outer layers of the body, forming a nerve net which conducts impulses which, in turn, cause muscular contractions.

Some flatworms show a further stage in the evolution of the nervous system, and the nerves are arranged in a ladderlike system in which the neurons are found in bundles known as nerve cords. The nerve cord is like a very rudimentary spinal cord. Also in the flatworm, the cell bodies of the neurons are concentrated in the head region, forming something very similar to a primitive brain. In this kind of nervous system, polarized synapses form junctions between the neurons, allowing impulses to travel in one direction only, an advance on the structure of the nerve net, in which impulses travel both ways.

From the flatworms and their simple synaptic nervous system, evolution followed two pathways in the formation of more complicated systems: the invertebrates, such as insects, following one path, and the vertebrates, later to include the cat family, following another. It is the latter path we shall follow.

First, however, it is important to know a little about the basic units of the nervous system, the neurons themselves, for these specialized cells hold the secrets of learning, memory and all mental functions. Each neuron has a nucleus, together with components found in other functional body cells. The cell body contains the nucleus, and from the body extend the dendrites which act as receivers to pick up activity from adjacent cells. The axon is a long fiber that extends from the cell body and transmits activity to other neurons, muscles or glands. The nerve impulses usually move in one direction from the dendrites, through the cell body, and along the axon to the dendrites of the next neuron, and so on, perhaps reaching a muscle or gland. Neurons all have the same general features, but can vary tremendously in shape and size. The neurons in the spinal cord, for example, may be very long indeed.

A nerve is made up of a bundle of elongated dendrites or axons from hundreds of neurons. The wiring system between the neurons is very complex and hundreds of axons may connect with the dendrites of one neuron. The synapses form the junction points, and are like minute fuse boxes, enabling the transmission of impulses in a very complex manner between the neurons forming the nerves. Transmissions are chemical, and it is a knowledge of this chemistry which enables anesthetics and analgesics to be effective, by blocking the transmission of impulses at the synaptic junctions.

Vertebrate brains evolved very slowly through the ages, first adapting through the most primitive of fishes, then through the reptiles, the birds and the early mammals. The cat's brain still shows characteristics found in the most primitive of brains. For example, the three enlargements known as the forebrain, the midbrain and the hindbrain are clearly defined. In the dogfish, a present-day sharklike animal very similar to the primitive fishes, an important feature of the brain is the olfactory bulb of the forebrain area which is chiefly concerned with the sense of smell, and the cerebrum, also in the forebrain, which uses the incoming smell information to influence the fish's behavior. Other important parts of the forebrain are the thalamus, concerned with dealing with impulses coming up from the spinal cord and down from the cerebrum, and the hypothalamus, which controls internal regulatory processes.

The midbrain is mainly made up of the optic lobes, and deals with and regulates behavior from the stimuli of sight. The hindbrain includes the cerebellum, which controls balance and coordination, and the medulla, the enlarged end of the spinal cord, which controls such vital functions as circulation and respiration. The comparative size of the various components of each species' brain is directly related to the life-style of that species. Organisms that rely heavily on scent to obtain food have large olfactory lobes, while those which need precise coordination, such as birds for flight, have large cerebellums.

As mammals evolved, so a more complex sensory system came into being, needing better centers for memory, learning and for problem solving. A new area of brain, known as the cerebral cortex, developed from an outgrowth of the cerebrum, forming a cover over it. In mammals of the lower orders this brain area, though well-developed, is smooth, while in those of the higher orders, including the cat, the surface is very wrinkled or convoluted, giving a greater surface area.

In the cat, the brain consists essentially of the structures of the more primitive brain, in similar anatomical relations but modified in detail, and it also has a very well-developed cerebral cortex overlying the older brain structures. The primitive core may still be found, the old brain or limbic system which evolved on the original core, and the new brain which evolved upon the old brain. All the sections are closely interdependent. The central core of the brain regulates the endocrine gland activity, and also controls metabolism and respiration and maintains homeostasis, which means that processes such as heart rate, blood pressure, temperature and blood-salts concentration all work at steady, controlled rates, worked by feedback mechanisms located in the hypothalamus.

Along the innermost edges of the cerebral hemispheres are parts of the brain which control more complex functions. These structures, known as the limbic system, control some respiratory and digestive functions, but also take care of activities requiring a strict sequential response, such as eating, mating or fleeing from danger. This system is vital for the survival of members of the cat family, for these instinctive activities must be carried out in their sequential manner to be totally effective.

The two large hemispheres at the top of the brain contain a very large proportion of all the neurons present. The hemispheres are symmetrical, with a deep division running between them from front to rear. The left hemisphere controls most of the functions of the right side of the body, while the right hemisphere controls the functions of the left side. The two hemispheres are connected, so that inputs can be correlated. This area of the brain controls the higher mental processes and the most flexible and least stereotyped aspects of behavior.

Different areas of the cortex control different parts of the cat's body. The front of the cortex controls the movements of the legs and extremities, an area of brain slightly farther back controls the body, while the rear portion of the brain has areas important to the visual sense. Auditory areas are found at the sides of the hemispheres. The cerebral cortex also houses the complex areas concerned with conscious sensation, learning, memory and activity.

The brain of today's pet cat bears a brain weight to body weight ratio of 1:99, whereas in the dog it is 1:235 and in the horse, 1:593. This would seem to give the cat a higher intelligence quotient than either the dog or the horse. In fact, intelligence depends not only on the weight of the brain, but also more on the proportions of gray and white matter present, and on the complexity of the synaptic junctions. Nevertheless, the cat has a highly developed and complex brain, very similar to that of man, and its intelligence and capacity for learning should not be underestimated.

Testing Your Cat's IQ

The intelligence tests devised by the French psychologist
Alfred Binet (1856–1911) were designed to detect children who were too slow or dull to benefit from schooling.
A scale of units was drawn up to correspond with *mental
age* (MA), and the ratio of this to the *chronological age* (CA),
multiplied by 100 to get rid of the decimal point, gave
the *intelligence quotient* (IQ):

$$IQ = 100 \times \frac{MA}{CA}$$

Thus, when MA is equal to CA, the IQ equals 100. If the MA is much less than the CA, the resulting IQ will be less than 100 and will indicate a dull subject, while an MA above the CA indicates a bright subject.

This test proved really satisfactory only for children between the ages of six and fifteen years. Eventually, refined tests were devised for human adults, the results of which were computed from tables allowing each age to average an IQ of 100 with a standard deviation of 16. This modern test score, adjusted to the age of the subject, is no longer a quotient at all, but the expression IQ has been retained for the sake of convenience.

In human IQ tests, seven factors known as primary abilities are explored. These are verbal comprehension, word fluency, number (simple arithmetic tests), space (drawing designs from memory), memory (recall of paired items), perceptual speed (grasping visual details of pictured objects) and reasoning (completion of a series, having been presented with only a small portion of that series). It is easy to see that there is no way that any of these seven factors can be tested in the domestic cat.

As we discussed in Chapter 2, the cat is an intelligent creature, having evolved through natural selection until the time of the Pharaohs. In nature, a mentally subnormal animal would not survive long. Since man's intervention in things, however, it is apparent that degrees of intelligence are recognizable in most species, not the least in man himself.

How are we to test the aptitude and ability of our own cats? We cannot test their vocabulary or their arithmetic ability; they cannot draw or write; and we cannot expect recall of paired nouns or any other results expected from ordinary IQ tests. To evaluate the cat's IQ we must first establish some sort of behavioral/intelligence norm. This can be achieved only by studying a large cross section of cats picked at random from all types of environments; cats of all ages—male, female and neuter. Set patterns of cat behavior and response can then be tabulated and analyzed. Eventually, a table of average, normal behavior and intelligence level can be drawn up. To test our own cat's IQ, it would then be a simple matter to obtain a copy of the standard for cat IQ and to subject our cat to a few simple tests to evaluate its adherence to or deviation from the norm. But what tests?

As we cannot expect our cat to answer us verbally, tests have to be devised in which its behavioral response will indicate that definite thought processes were used. We also need to study in detail the cat's response mechanisms; for instance, expressions of the eyes, pupil dilation and movement indicate various emotions and responses in the cat. Whisker and tail twitching, ear placement and movement, mewing and growling and the erection of body and tail hair are obvious indicators of response to stimuli.

Memory can be tested by observation quite easily, and perhaps we should start by devising some feline memory tests. Show your hungry cat its favorite food in a conspicuous dish. While it watches, have it held as you place the dish on a shelf or some other accessible but unusual place in the room. Then, take the cat outside and interest it in some other form of favorite activity for a while. What does it do when it is taken back to the room where the food is placed? Does it remember where you put the food and go straight there? Or does it go to its usual site, sniff around and eventually find it by scent? If your cat does go straight to the food, is this really a test of memory, or does it just have a particularly well-developed "nose"? To control the sense of smell in this experiment, one would have to block the nose of the cat, and it would probably be so irritated by this that it would not bother to look for its dinner anyway.

The same sort of experiment can be performed with a favorite toy. After you have played exciting tossing games with its best catnip mouse, hold the cat, place the mouse under a cushion or rug while your pet looks on. Take the cat from the room and distract its attention for a while, then let it back in to see if it immediately seeks out the toy. If it does, does this prove that it is extraintelligent or does it just have a good memory?

One good test is often performed by those fortunate people who are owned by several cats. With all the pets relaxed in one room, call the animals' names softly, one by one, and each particular cat should respond as its name is spoken. Again, this is questionable as a measure of intelligence, for even the dullest of cats may be taught to answer to its name, having been conditioned by being called for meals and the food acting as a reward and thus a reinforcer.

Another test easily performed in the home is to place the cat in a room with a heavy door separating it from its owner. The cat is watched by an observer, while the owner makes dinnertime noises and calls the cat. A dull cat will push the door at the base, and when it does not immediately open, will run to and fro in an agitated manner looking for another way out. The intelligent cat will push the door at the base, then, failing to open it, will stand up and push it a little higher for extra leverage. The superintelligent cat will back off and take a run at the door, but as far as it has been possible to ascertain, this behavior has not been observed.

An overall study of individual cats should give a better assessment of their intelligence than the application of tests. IQ tests, even in human subjects, do not measure persistence, and a persistent cat may succeed, for example, in a food-attainment test, when a more intelligent cat has given up to try a different tack. Escape-type tests do not really test intelligence either. In this situation, anxiety can play a strong motivating part, and a highly anxious cat is more likely to escape from a puzzle box or maze than is an intelligent but very relaxed cat.

Practice and coaching can also improve test scores in laboratory situations, so it follows that a dull cat, having had lots of time to learn a task, even if it is quite a complicated one, would perform it better than a highly intelligent cat trying the task for the first time. Criteria standardization is therefore of utmost importance in setting up IQ tests for your cat.

Perhaps your cat is just a cat. He is a family pet, neutered and in good health. He comes and goes as he pleases, he knows his mealtimes and sits waiting by the wall can opener at the appropriate times, a happy expression on his face, perhaps kneading with his forepaws, or rubbing his face and body against your legs or the furniture. He refuses to do any tricks, and any attempt to make him perform or to look ridiculous in any way results in low growling and a stilted walk offstage, tail lightly flashing from side to side. When in the boarding cattery, he goes on a hunger strike for two or three days and sulks a bit when he is brought home again. If allowed to roam the garden, he occasionally stalks birds, fallen leaves or waving grasses. He likes to sit in the warmth, on the best chair in the evenings, and purrs when he is stroked. He is just a normal, happy, intelligent cat; why should you care how he would score in an IQ test?

Maybe your cat is not just an ordinary cat; his pedigree may not be merely a list of similar forebears but the result of careful breeding by a total-points-score system whereby a dedicated breeder has assessed the breeding stock not only for looks, but also for other important traits such as tractability and a high degree of intelligent behavior. Such a cat does not need IQ testing to show that he has that little bit extra. He will be able to open latched doors by the handles, soon working out the amount of body swing necessary to move the door once the latch is depressed. He will sit on your knee when you relax, disappear when you feel agitated and watch you serenely from the mat when you feel blue. He will soon be able to open the refrigerator door, know all the most comfortable places to sleep—on top of the television when it is on, in the linen closet and on your bed just after you have left it. He will know on which days noisy callers call, and will hide when the garbage men arrive. He will growl at dogs in the garden, make juddering noises at birds, but not bother to chase them, and will have you firmly under his paw.

The dull cat will sit in the rain and howl outside the back door to be let in, and if you do not hear will continue to sit and howl until thoroughly soaked. The bright cat will go around the house, find out which room you are in and then howl on that windowsill. Dull cats fight when you have to give them pills and medicines, while intelligent ones trust you enough to allow the dosing. Dull cats loathe riding in cars and may vanish when they see the cat carrier being fetched. Bright cats like to be with their owners, even in cars. They do not like to be boarded out, and need extra care in catteries with much fuss and attention and lots of conversation. Extremely intelligent cats hide the moment they see the suitcases appear and the activity of packing commence.

Dull cats get their heads stuck inside cans; bright cats use their paws to scoop food from narrow-necked containers. Dull cats get stuck up trees and down rabbit holes; intelligent ones do, too, but manage to unstick themselves as soon as they find no one is taking any notice of their wailing. Do dull cats become road casualties more often than bright cats? Who knows? Maybe the bright ones look right, then left, then right again, but no statistics are available. Are bright cats more prone to heart disease or stress than dull cats? Again, no one seems to know.

For laboratory work, cats are specially bred and are of similar genetic background. They are reared in similar environments and treated in like manner. Thus, all possible variables are removed before tests on various reactions and brain responses are made. Our own cats come from all sorts of sources. They may be reared in any one of a hundred different ways, so there are far too many variables present for any serious form of intelligence testing.

Having studied your cat, therefore, and assessed him as best you can against the best norm you have been able to draw upon expected behavioral responses, you could give the norm an arbitrary score of, say, 100, and score your own cat accordingly a few points above or below the 100 mark. If it comes off rather badly in the performance rating, does not bother to try to open doors, does not come when called, ignores your moods and, perhaps, has the occasional lapse of manners on the carpet, it may not mean that it merits a score of only 80 or so. It could mean that it is performing its own series of tests on you and that its own score is really in the region of 120 or more!

The Cat Is an Organism

The cat is a flesh-and-blood organism, a mammal, closely related to other organisms, including man, through its evolutionary history. Its habits, functions and actions are controlled by its brain and nervous system, and in order to study and hope to understand its behavioral patterns to any degree, one must begin with a clear understanding of that nervous system and the related structures of sense organs, muscles and glands.

By one's studying the bodily processes, in particular the

action of the brain, the areas of behavior that can be more clearly understood are those of sensory discrimination, regulatory, need-serving and emotional behavior, including eating, sleeping, fighting, fleeing and mating.

To be termed an "organism" implies that the cat is an organized structure in which the collection of cells is arranged into functional organs and organ systems. To understand the behavior of the cat, one has to know how the organs and related systems work. Voluntary acts are carried out smoothly with the cooperation of involuntary reflexes; emotions are aroused and followed by set patterns of behavior; information is received and dealt with by the animal; and although the mind deals with mental processes, it is the body that gives expression to mental activity. We shall therefore begin by looking at the makeup of the cat's body.

Muscles and the skeleton of the cat are its mechanical integrators. The body operates effectively as a machine mainly because of the way in which it is constructed around a jointed skeleton of rigid bones. This mode of construction makes it possible for the cat to maintain posture, to have varied speeds of locomotion, varied facial and bodily expressions and a limited vocabulary. The skeleton is overlaid by muscles.

When muscles contract, movement is effected in one or more joints, and gives rise to movements such as leaping, walking or running. Muscles may contract and the joints be prevented from moving, keeping the animal in an alert though quiet state. This amount of contraction is known as muscle tone, and in healthy cats, receiving plenty of exercise, this tone will be high, while in fat, weak or listless cats, the tone will be low. When muscle tone is reduced too far, as in the case of a serious, debilitating illness, the animal may die. Sometimes, as a result of an injury during birth, the muscle tone may be too high, resulting in a spastic condition, making smooth muscle movement impossible.

Muscle tone is maintained automatically through the natural reflexes of the cat, but sometimes cats increase the tone deliberately, such as by stretching to a great extent after a catnap by the fire. Cats in a highly emotional state, often when at a cat show or while at boarding kennels, may tense their muscles for long periods, causing fatigue and a low resistance to infection. Mild personality disturbances may occur during these periods, causing usually friendly cats to bite and scratch, and the lowering of resistance to infection allows viral infections to take hold, in many cases following shows or holiday periods.

The cat may voluntarily increase the tension of antagonistic muscles. These are arranged in pairs and the contraction of one member of the pair tends to stretch the other member. In the case of the shoulder and forearm of the cat, the biceps is a flexor muscle pulling the leg forward and upward to make a step, while the triceps is an extensor muscle, acting in an antagonistic way to the biceps and pulling the leg straight again, thus propelling the animal forward. Muscles usually work in this manner and when one of the pair contracts, the other usually relaxes. This simple principle is known as reciprocal innervation.

Reciprocal innervation comes into play whenever the cat is moving its muscles in an involuntary manner—taking a stroll around the garden, getting up in the morning, running from danger or climbing trees. It enables the cat to be fully coordinated in all its actions and to maintain an alertness at all times.

A second and equally important system of control in the cat is that of the circulation, and includes the functioning of the heart, blood vessels and other closely linked structures. The circulatory system is chemical in its action, and supplements the mechanical integration of the muscles and joints.

The bloodstream carries important activators around the body, discharged into the blood from the ductless glands. The activators are known as hormones and have effects on growth, personality and behavior, and are important in this study of the behavior of the cat.

Ductless or endocrine glands secrete the hormones, each gland or pair of glands having a specific function. There are two pituitary glands: the anterior one controls growth and acts as a "master" gland, influencing the secretions from the thyroid, pancreas, adrenals and the gonads; the posterior pituitary controls water metabolism. The thyroid gland controls the metabolic rate, and, therefore, activity and fatigue, as well as tendencies to fatness or thinness. The thymus regulates the lymphoid system and causes the development of immune reactions in the body. The parathyroid controls the metabolism of calcium and helps to maintain normal levels of nervous excitement. The pancreas, through insulin release, controls the sugar metabolism system. There are two parts to the adrenal glands: the cortex area controls the metabolism of salt and carbohydrate, while the medulla area is active in emotion. The gonads, as glands of internal secretion as distinguished from their reproductive functions, give rise to secondary sex characteristics, such as the jowly effect seen in the tomcat and the enlarging of the breasts in the pregnant queen.

The adrenal cortex hormones are so important to the life of the cat that the destruction of this gland invariably leads to death. If certain glands fail, it is possible, in some cases, to replace the hormones they would normally secrete by complex chemical substances known as steroids, given by injection or by mouth. Many illnesses have been successfully treated by means of steroid therapy, but odd behavioral symptoms have been observed in some cats after long courses of steroids such as cortisone.

A third system, the neural mechanism, controls the mechanical and chemical integrators that we have looked at, for it controls the muscles using the skeleton, and also controls the heartbeat, respiration and circulation, as well as the gland secretions. The possession of a nervous system enables the organism, in this case the cat, to be capable of very complex and modifiable action. It provides the means for learning from experiences and for adaptation to changes in the environment, and therefore deserves a chapter to itself.

The Cat's Nervous System

As we have seen, the central nervous system of the cat, consisting of the brain and spinal cord, is the animal's "head office," and controls and coordinates all its activities, constantly monitoring all information for degrees of importance. Some is discarded, some is stored in the memory for future use and some is acted upon immediately.

The nerves which lie outside the spinal cord are termed peripheral, and throughout most of their length in the cat's body, they contain mixed fibers. The incoming or afferent fibers carry information from the whiskers, skin, pads, muscles and joints to the spinal cord; it is then transmitted to the brain. The outgoing or efferent fibers convey return messages sent from the motor region of the brain, through the spinal cord to muscle fibers, causing the muscles to react. Each area of the cat's body has a corresponding section of the spinal cord which receives and gives nerve messages. These peripheral nerves are often called somatic nerves because they act upon and innervate the striated body muscles attached to the skeleton.

Nerves which control self-regulating activities such as digestion and circulation, which go on even during the cat's sleeping periods, form the autonomic nervous system. This system has two clear divisions, which are often antagonistic in their actions, and are known as the sympathetic and parasympathetic fibers. The first type of fiber acts as a unit. For example, if the cat is emotionally aroused the sympathetic system simultaneously speeds up the heart rate, dilates the arteries of both heart and muscles to increase the blood flow and constricts the arteries of the skin and internal organs. Hormones are released into the bloodstream and the animal is poised and ready for action.

The parasympathetic system acts in a piecemeal manner and affects one organ at a time. It participates in digestive functions and conserves and stores bodily resources. Occasionally the two divisions of the autonomic system may operate together, and sometimes they are called upon to work in sequence. For example, in the complete sex act of the male cat it is the parasympathetic function which causes erection, while the sympathetic function causes ejaculation.

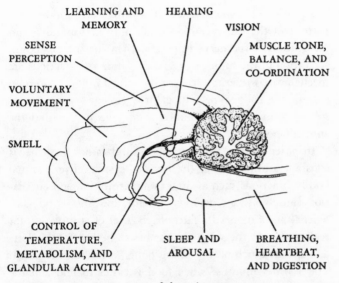

LEARNING AND
MEMORY

HEARING

VISION

SENSE
PERCEPTION

MUSCLE TONE,
BALANCE, AND
CO-ORDINATION

VOLUNTARY
MOVEMENT

SMELL

CONTROL OF
TEMPERATURE,
METABOLISM, AND
GLANDULAR ACTIVITY

SLEEP AND
AROUSAL

BREATHING,
HEARTBEAT,
AND DIGESTION

Association areas of the cat's nervous system

In the cat, the autonomic nervous system is particularly well developed, for, being a solitary animal, it relies on its own powers of fight and flight for survival, in direct contrast to the dog, which has the combined responses of the pack for protection and survival in the wild. This difference in cat and dog accounts for the way most pet animals react in the veterinarian's office. The dog, though possibly alarmed, accepts treatment calmly, while many cats need firm, experienced handling before medication can be given. It also helps to explain why many more stray cats survive and go feral than do abandoned dogs. The cat can cope in its solitary way, and often goes unnoticed, while the dog, requiring a pack life for survival, is soon caught and taken to the pound.

As in man, responsiveness to stimulation follows a set pattern in the cat: reception of stimuli, transmission and integration of the nerve impulses, then the corresponding activation of the muscles or glands. Some reflex actions are mechanical; for example, gentle scratching at a certain part of the cat's spine will elicit a violent scratching response from a hind leg aimed at an area just behind the animal's neck.

In order to stay healthy in body and mind, a cat needs constant stimulation of the nervous system. Even normal bodily functions such as digestion, respiration and circulation cause constant nervous activity, but this is not sufficient, and cats need a fairly high level of stimulation for real fitness. In the wild, the cat has to be constantly alert, and spends much of its waking hours in the hunt for food. The warmer months, when food is easier to find and the cat expends less energy, are the season for the wildcat to reproduce itself, and so the level of nervous awareness is constantly maintained. If a cat is kept for long periods in isolation or under conditions of very restricted stimulation, such as in a badly designed boarding cattery consisting of small, viewless cubicles, quite severe disturbances in perception will be seen. The cat, on returning home, may have difficulty in judging distances, may fall when jumping up or down, and may well knock into objects. A stud male should never be kept in an isolated shed, but must have plenty to look at and large runs for exercise. The owner must spend some time with him each day, grooming him and playing with him, or his personality and performance will suffer.

Small kittens and house cats also need stimulation, and

should not be left alone for long hours in a normal, tidy room. They should have plenty of toys, or preferably, another animal as a companion. They should be encouraged to look out from the windowsill and should be handled and played with whenever possible if denied the freedom of the garden. The understimulated cat, though it may be adjusted to its own environment, will violently resist handling when it is removed from it, for it will overreact to any stimulation it then receives and will prove virtually impossible to treat medically or to board out.

Overstimulation places the cat under as great a strain as understimulation, so it is important to strike a happy balance with the pet cat. By taking a wild animal and domesticating it over the centuries, we also take on the responsibility of compensating it for its loss of natural environment and responses. By providing food we remove a need to hunt, by neutering we remove the need to reproduce, by keeping the animal in the house we remove its need to keep warm—indeed, it is surprising that the cat has remained as well-balanced and tractable a pet as we find it today.

When the cat is overstimulated, its mechanisms can no longer function normally, and if the stresses continue, permanent damage may be caused, or even death. Infection, extremes of heat or cold, nervous strain, physical injury or fatigue can all place the cat under conditions of great stress, and it is when the stress is prolonged that the situation becomes serious. Situations in which stress causes illness will be found at various points in this book, but it must be remembered that a little stress is necessary at all stages in the life of the cat; it is only when the stress level becomes too much that trouble ensues. The cat first receives stimulation, or is stressed, at the moment of birth. The tiny kitten has to fight for the nipple and later compete for solid food with its siblings. It learns contentment and fear, experiences warmth and cold, light and darkness, hears loud and sudden noises. All this is normal stimulation and helps to form synaptic junctions in the tiny brain. A kitten kept at a constant temperature in the dark will find it difficult to adapt when it ventures forth at six weeks, for it will have been understimulated and will have little perceptive power. It may be underdeveloped mentally for the rest of its life.

A normally stimulated, happy, healthy cat is a successful creature with excellent powers of sight, smell, hearing, taste and touch. Its nervous system is alerted by receptors in the eyes, nose, ears and other sense organs, and the messages are transmitted along the afferent fibers to the spinal cord and into the brain for processing. Then the corresponding response is sent back down the spinal cord and along the efferent fibers to effectors in the correct muscles for the required action to take place.

Homeostasis works in the cat to ensure that a balance is maintained during normal conditions between over- and understimulation by constant interaction between glands and a complex feedback monitoring system present for this very purpose. It is only in abnormal conditions that stress factors get out of hand.

The Cat's Senses and Reflexes

Most cat owners believe that their pets have a sixth sense, but whether this is true or not, cats certainly possess the usual five senses, each of which is highly developed.

The eyes of the cat consist of a pair of eyeballs from which optic nerves lead to the brain. Each eyeball is spherical, with a protective window, the cornea, at the front. An aperture called the pupil is centered in the cornea and allows light to pass through the lens to focus onto a light-sensitive area, the retina. The pupil enlarges and contracts to allow varying amounts of light to enter. In bright light the pupil will appear as a narrow slit, while in semidarkness it will open until it almost fills the aperture of the eye. The lens is also able to contract and extend itself, thus providing a greater extent of clear vision than found in some other mammals.

Light passes through the lens and converges, forming an image on the retina, which, in the cat, is covered by a special reflecting membrane to ensure that every available detail is conserved, and to allow for excellent vision even in conditions of semidarkness. This reflecting membrane gives rise to the phenomenon most of us have seen, when the eyes of cats or foxes reflect the distant glare of headlights in a quiet lane. It also accounts for the disappointing photographs many of us have taken using flashbulbs, when the prints show the eyes of the cat as large yellow or red balls of reflected light.

The field of vision in the cat has a large amount of overlap. This is because the eyes are set on the front of the head, typical of the eye set of a predator. The cat has binocular vision, which enables its brain to make a very accurate assessment and judgment of the position of its prey, and which aids in accurate negotiation of difficult terrain and in jumping and climbing. In the cat the eye has the usual rods, easily stimulated and effective even in dim light conditions. It also has cones which are sensitive to light of various wavelengths, which leads one to suppose that cats can perceive some colors, even if not the spectrum which can be perceived by man. The cat's eye is very adaptable, having an enormous variation in pupil contraction, and it is further protected by a third eyelid, or nictitating membrane, which shutters the eye from the inside edge, under the two normal eyelids.

Smell is very important to the cat and is very well developed. The young kitten learns which smells indicate wholesome, nontoxic foods, and for this reason it is very important to feed kittens on very varied diets, for, if not, they may accept only a limited range of foods as adults. The taste buds do not seem so important to the cat. The receptor cells of the nose are highly specialized and are covered with minute projections called olfactory hairs which increase the surface area of the receptor cells. These also increase the chances of an odorous substance being detected by the cat and being relayed to the brain.

In the hard palate, just behind the upper incisors, the cat has two tiny ducts which lead to the vomeronasal, or Jacobson's, organ. When smelling certain substances, a strange cat or catnip, for instance, the cat will open its mouth and stretch its neck high and may even gulp a little, allowing the smell to be drawn up into the organ. This curious behavior is known as the flehmen reaction, and although it is known to have sexual and aggressive significance in rabbits, little is known about its significance in cats.

Smell is the first of the senses to be used by the newborn kitten. Blind and helpless, it nevertheless locates the nipple by smell alone. Sometimes when kittens are born, amniotic fluid is present in the nostrils. Unless this is cleared, the kitten may inhale the fluid and pneumonia will later develop, and it will be unable to locate a nipple to feed upon. Placing the kitten to a nipple will be unsuccessful, for it is the smell, and the smell alone, which triggers the nursing impulse.

The sense of smell is also very important in the reproduction of the cat, as the smell of a queen in estrus excites the male into mating condition. Cats also indulge in territorial marking by spraying the limits of their home range with droplets of urine. Some chemical substances are very attractive to cats; they will stop to sniff at plants containing the chemical, savor the smell and then may roll and stretch ecstatically along the ground. Plants particularly liked by cats are catnip, *Nepeta cataria,* valerian, *Valeriana officinalis* and cat thyme, *Teucrium marum.* Cats eat only freshly killed meat, or its present-day equivalent of newly opened canned food, and most find carrion, or decaying food, wholly repugnant.

The ear of the cat consists of a well-designed, forward-pointing pinna. The pinna is mobile and can turn toward sounds. Having two ears makes the source of sound easy to locate, and the tiny noises made by creatures such as field mice can be picked up easily by the alert cat. Sound is also a powerful sexual stimulant, and the call of a queen in season attracts male cats from miles around. Most cats quickly learn their own names and will respond to them. Owners of several cats should pick names quite dissimilar in sound; an effective party trick can then be performed where each pet in turn can respond, as it is quietly called. Cats do not seem to like high-pitched noises, and some pets have been known to become quite agitated at the sound of a violin or high-flying jet aircraft overhead.

The receptors for touch, warmth and cold are distributed over the whole of the skin area, some areas having clusters of receptors and thus being more sensitive than others. Many receptors are present around the hairs of the coat, and are clustered in certain regions, which explains the pleasure given to the cat by stroking, especially around

Male cat adopting a typically aggressive position, sideways onto an adversary, tail hairs erect, head in striking position and performing much lip-smacking to scare away the threatening visitor. (*Animal Graphics*)

Blue Himalayan male adopting a defensive attitude, having marked his territorial boundary. (*Animal Graphics*)

A Tabby and White *(left)* yawns and stretches, extending its claws. Cats invariably stretch their claws fully as part of the awakening process. *(Animal Graphics)*

A Havana queen protectively watching her kittens, aged four–five weeks, on their first exploratory trip from the nest box.
(Animal Graphics)

Kitten at play, tail catching. The tail is often indicative of the cat's state of mind. It can show fear, pleasure, and the animal's determination to stalk a prey. *(Hugh Smith)*

Poise

Taking off

A study of grace and coordination in a Siamese cat. *(Hugh Smith)*

Agility

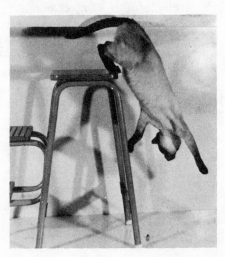

Twist descent

Two kittens will play together for hours on end and provide much more pleasure for the owner than a single kitten. Here the Siamese kittens are after a goldfish. *(Hugh Smith)*

Play behavior is important to the young kitten, and simple toys often provide the most exciting games. Here a paper bag with a torn corner becomes a den and even incites the older cat to join the game. *(Hugh Smith)*

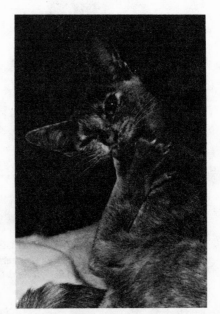

Cats are fastidious in their toilet and clean even their extremities thoroughly each day. They are without doubt the cleanest of domestic pets.
(Hugh Smith)

Cats, when excited, often make strange noises. This always fascinates a companion who listens with care but does not join in. *(Paul Bookbinder/Animal Graphics)*

Mutual grooming as seen between these two Blue Burmese is common between friendly cats in the same household. *(Paul Bookbinder/Animal Graphics)*

the head and chin. The vibrissae, or whiskers, are extrasensitive, very specialized hairs which protect the cat's face and eyes from damage. A flick on the whiskers gives rise to an almost simultaneous protective eye blink. An inquisitive cat, exploring new terrain, holds the whisker pads bunched up, the whiskers pointing forward and outward, obviously indicating that these are used to test for danger.

Taste is not very important to the cat, but well-remembered tastes, associated with well-remembered smells, enable the cat, before eating, to analyze its food for nutritional value and freedom from toxic substances. Taste buds are present in the mouth of the cat, and the animal can distinguish between salts, acids, bitterness and fresh water. The cat does not seem to be able to distinguish between sweet and nonsweet foods, and does not appreciate sugar or chocolate as does the pet dog.

Survival of the fittest in the wild in days gone by has ensured that the present-day cat has fantastic reflex action. The flexion reflexes in the legs are very refined, enabling the cat to walk a narrow span girder thousands of feet in the air without falling, to traverse a mantelpiece covered with priceless china without upsetting one piece and to walk on sharp gravel without tearing its delicate pads. The self-correcting reflex is, perhaps, the one for which the cat is best known. This is an extension of a very primitive reflex, found even in very low-order animals, which enables them to turn right side up when placed on their backs. In the cat dropped upside down from a height, many senses immediately come into play, including information from the complicated labyrinth in the inner ear.

Movement of the fluid in the series of tiny tubes tells the brain which way the body is held in relation to the earth. When dropped, a series of set, coordinated movements are performed instinctively by the cat, causing it to land safely on its four feet.

Behavior and Learning
in the Kitten

As we have seen, the newborn kitten is blind and deaf and moves by crawling, belly touching the ground, toward the mother's nipple, guided only by the strongly developed sense of smell. Weak kittens are stimulated by the mother, who uses firm strokes of her rough tongue to clean away traces of the birth sac and amniotic fluid from the kitten's fur, and in doing so promotes its circulation and respiration. Each kitten in the litter appears to have a preference for a particular nipple, which it will endeavor to suckle right through the nursing stage. Quite strong and determined scrabbling movements can be observed in the new litter, as the stronger kittens try to assert their claims on their particular nipple. While suckling, the kittens use their tiny paws, kneading either side of the teat to help the milk flow, and this treading, kneading action becomes stronger as the kittens grow.

Evacuation of the bowel and bladder is stimulated by the mother's licking of the genital area for the first three or four weeks, and she swallows all traces of the feces and urine. In the wild, this would prevent the nest from becoming soiled and thus attracting predators by the smell. When the kittens start eating solid food, the queen ceases to ingest the wastes and the kittens learn to move away from the nest to empty themselves.

Immediately following the birth, the kittens prefer to sleep in one particular spot in the nest box, and will be stressed if moved from it. Many owners of breeding queens take great trouble to remove every trace of soiled paper or blanket from the box, replacing it with a spotlessly clean blanket. This might well be the cause of neuroses in many adult cats. The unique smell imparted to the nest during birth is the only "homing" scent that the kittens have in their first few days of life. Remove the soiled areas, which, incidentally, cannot be termed "dirty," for the secretions of labor and birth are totally sterile, and you remove a smell which gives the kitten security.

At birth, the neurons of the brain that will last through life are already present. Brain cells are never renewed. All mammals start with millions and these gradually decay through the life span. The brain of the kitten is already very functional, but the more synaptic junctions which form in the first few weeks of its life, the more intelligent will be the adult cat. Stressing helps brain development, and so the kittens should be handled from birth onward. Experiments have proved that extra handling during the first four weeks of life produces more intelligent cats than does leaving them alone in a dark, secluded nest box until weaning time. Stressed kittens open their eyes early, are more sociable and will be toddling from the nest much sooner than ignored kittens, but stressing should not be taken to mean rough handling. At first, your merely picking the kitten up gently and letting it smell your strange clothes or face will be sufficiently stimulating.

During the development of new colors in pedigreed cats, for years it had been noticed that it was the odd-colored kittens in each litter that grew up to be superintelligent, tractable and healthy cats, and this fact was put down to some sort of hybrid vigor. Only later, and after study of psychology, was it realized that it was the extra handling from birth the unusual kittens received that produced the supercats. The appearance of a kitten exhibiting the desired new shade in a mixed litter would mean that the exciting little creature was examined at birth to determine its sex. It was probably given a good rub with a small piece of rough toweling to ensure that its lungs were clear of fluid and that its circulation was going strong. It was handled each day to make certain that there was no sepsis of the navel developing and that its eyes were opening normally. All this handling and examination are very stressful to a newborn kitten and cause early maturation of the brain's activity.

The age of four to eight weeks appears to be a critical period in the kitten's life, when it needs to be socialized with humans if it is to be calm, and to like handling as an adult cat. This period coincides with the nest-leaving time in the wild, and this is when wild kittens would learn which are their friends and enemies. Kittens should be handled a great deal at this age; they should have their ears gently wiped out, their teeth and feet inspected so that this is accepted procedure later. Very gentle grooming with a baby brush is appreciated, and will elicit quite strong purring.

During the critical socializing period, it is important for kittens to meet children and dogs as well as adults and other cats. Also, it is a good time to introduce them to the noises of the household that they will encounter later in life—for example, the washing machine and vacuum cleaner. Rides in the car can be taken if the kitten is safely contained in a warm carrier. All these stressful procedures, though mildly traumatic at the time, will help the kitten to grow into a well-adjusted, intelligent adult, adaptable to most environments.

Kittens raised in large catteries, seeing humans only at feeding or cleaning-up times, remain rather shy of human contact and are often difficult to handle by the veterinarian and at cat shows, although they may become very attached to their owners. The orphan kitten, on the other hand, raised by a human foster mother from birth, may become a worse problem if it is not introduced to other cats during the critical period, for it grows up to be overhumanized. A kitten was reared in this way, fed with formula by syringe from birth, by a breeder who was recovering from a serious illness and who was pleased to have this absorbing task to perform. The kitten lived in the breeder's room for the first ten weeks of her life and was a delight, being superaffectionate, clean and dainty in her habits. She purred for the vet while being vaccinated and eventually went to a new home where she settled in, adored by her new mistress and the children of the house.

This kitten was a new variety of Siamese and a very good specimen, so her owner decided that she would breed from her when she matured. Eventually, the little queen came into season and was taken to a stud male. On being placed in the queen's pen she caught sight of the male cat and became very agitated, climbing the wire of the pen and urinating. When attempts were made to get hold of her, she fought, biting and scratching, obviously thinking she was being attacked by the male. Eventually, she was calmed and returned home, and when she came into season again, another attempt was made to introduce her to the male. Despite being quite frantically in heat and being left for three days in the warm, secluded queen's pen where she could see and smell the male without direct contact, she was impossible to handle and would not mate. It was then realized that she had never seen other cats during her kittenhood, and only the occasional visiting human neighbor, at whom she hissed and spat, during her adult life—in fact, she did not know that she was a cat. It was obvious she would never mate and eventually she was spayed, living out her long life as a happy, neutered pet.

During the early days in the nest, the kitten will spend most of its time suckling and sleeping. Its eyes open between two and ten days, depending on the breed of cat and the light conditions, and its sense of hearing develops very gradually. Crawling then becomes stronger, and the kitten finds its way around the nest, pushing its nose along the ground and using scent as its guide. At this stage, the belly is in contact with the ground and its legs push the little animal forward, leaving scent trails around the nest.

After the eyes open, the first signs of play behavior may be seen as the kittens pat at each other. Sight is weak at first, but after a few days the kittens may be seen to focus on one another and look at the mother. By three weeks of age, the kittens can stand quite well and take tottering steps. They lick their paws, roll onto their backs and right themselves, and play, pawing at each other's faces and bodies and occasionally trying to bite at tails and paws. As they grow stronger, play becomes fiercer. Little excursions from the nest box are extended daily until daring sorties are made around the room. Sudden noises cause a dash for the safety of home and mother. During the first excursions, the sense of taste is explored by the kitten, which will lick most objects it encounters, and will lick quite vigorously at the floor. Many objects encountered will be tested by chewing and biting, and the nest box, if cardboard, will soon bear the impression of many needlelike teeth.

The kitten's brain is almost fully mature, with all its synaptic junctions formed and working, by the age of five weeks. But the kitten's motor development, the coordination of limbs and development of muscles, takes much longer. However, it has not learned discrimination at this age, and needs care to protect it from climbing onto dangerously high objects, from falling, from taking in toxic substances or from getting wet or burned. At this age it must have freedom to exercise with its littermates as much as possible, and also it should have plenty of toys and unusual objects to play with and explore. Various sorts of food should be offered at this age, so that a range of tastes develops, and the kitten should be placed firmly on a litter box after each eating or nursing session.

Territorial Marking and Communication

Entire male cats have an unpleasant habit of spraying their territory as often as possible. They do this by aiming a fine spray of urine against any conspicuous object, such as a fence, post or shrub, having turned their backs on the chosen item, and treading delicately in turn with the hind feet, tail erect and quivering. If kept indoors, toms will probably spray the furnishings also, and thus provide a good case in favor of neutering.

The urine of the entire male contains a thick, fatty substance which holds the unique tomcat odor, sticking it to the area marked, and lasting through washing, scrubbing, rain, sleet or hail. The mark acts as a calling card, and if another male wanders into the territory, he can sniff, be aware that he is in another's area, and either stay and await the consequences, or leave, avoiding trouble.

Cats also mark spots by other means, for they have scent glands on the lips and chin, on either side of the forehead and along the tail. The glands on the sides of the forehead are called the temporal glands. Any cat lover will agree that these are used often when the cat rubs its head in a friendly manner against one's legs or into the hand, eliciting a head-stroke, or against one's shoulder if being nursed. Cats also rub their heads against other cats in the same household, and this action smears a tiny amount of secretion from the gland onto the area they have rubbed. In fact, they are "marking" their friends by this method.

A similar form of rubbing, and therefore marking, is carried out with the lips and chin, where the secretions from the perioral gland are situated. The cat seems to find great pleasure in rubbing the sides of its lips against objects such as chair legs, and if another cat known to it has previously rubbed there, it seems to get even more pleasure from the action, often purring and tail waving at the same time. A cat has been seen to be so ecstatic over finding another friendly cat's "mark" that it rubs its own lips and chin so vigorously against the object that it rears up onto its hind legs, drools and marks with forehead and tail areas as well.

Often, after spraying an area with urine, a male cat will turn and strop the sprayed areas with his claws. At other times he may back up to the sprayed object and rub his tail and quarters against it. Some female cats and neuters spray occasionally, but not habitually as do the entire males. Spraying behavior is greatly increased if a strange cat has visited the area, and a normally house-clean male cat may spray the curtains and furniture if a new kitten is introduced to the household. A formerly house-clean neuter sometimes regresses through jealousy and starts spraying behavior on the introduction of a new kitten or a new baby, and while his spray will not be as noxious as that of the entire male, it must be discouraged at the outset so that it does not become habitual. Queens generally spray only when in estrus and very frustrated, using the male urinating position rather than the normal squatting position. Sometimes the giving of contraceptive pills to females has the effect of considerably upsetting the hormone balance, and spraying behavior follows.

As we shall see later, in Chapter 15, cats have a wide variety of facial expressions and bodily postures with which they are able to communicate not only with other cats but also with their human associates. A study of these expressions helps us to understand our pet cats better and leads to an ideal two-way relationship from the outset. The cat uses its head, body, eyes and tail to express itself, as well as its voice, and the various permutations of the positions of the parts of the body form an explicit language. Body postures and the voice are used together and sometimes in sequence to get the messages across.

Take the normal, nonaggressive cat, who sees a threat in the garden, perhaps in the form of another invading cat or maybe a dog. First the cat will "freeze," standing perfectly still, while it looks at the intruder; its tail may lightly flick from side to side and its ears and whiskers point forward, all senses straining to identify the threat. As the intruder gets a little closer, the cat's tail lifts slightly away from its back, its tip still pointing downward and its chin will be lowered, ears flattened, and it will begin to turn sideways, the hairs on body and tail starting to erect. This increasingly offensive display will continue if the intruder continues to approach, and when it is very near, the cat will be in its fully offensive position—hind legs tensed to spring, body turned to one side from the chest, the weight of the front body poised on one leg while the other, claws unsheathed, is raised and ready to strike. The chin is tucked well into the chest and the ears are flattened against the head. The lips will be drawn back and the cat will snarl furiously.

At this point, the intruder will usually back off a few steps and the cat will come forward, growling even more ferociously, the fluffed tail lashing from side to side. There may be some lip-smacking and drooling at this stage, which usually proves too much for the intruder, who turns tail and runs off. The cat will then sniff at the area invaded, may spray, defecate or scratch at it, then resume its normal, everyday constitutional.

A cat seeing another friendly cat approach acts in quite a different manner. First, the inquisitive ear-and-whiskers-forward stance is adopted, then when the familiar smell reaches it, its tail will rise straight up, it will bow its head slightly and walk slightly stiff-legged toward its friend, and they will greet each other by touching noses, and may, if very fond of each other, indulge in a little mutual grooming. Friendly cats often indulge in play, even when adult. They will chase each other in mock battle, turning sharply and hissing; and then one will run off until caught and bowled over, when the other will take its turn to be the chaser. Often, during games, cats will shin rapidly up trees, then suddenly turn in a very surprised fashion on finding themselves so far above the ground. They often cry for help in getting down, but if left alone, ease themselves back to ground level without any trouble.

The facial expressions are easy to understand in the cat. An alert cat, weighing the situation, looks directly at you with ears forward, whiskers slightly forward, perhaps with nostrils twitching if it is slightly nervous. Your reassuring voice will calm it, and the expression in its eyes will soften if it accepts you; its ears will relax slightly and it may emit a low cry or even purr. It is then safe to extend your hand.

If the ears are held slightly sideways and the eyes are open wide, perhaps looking rapidly from left to right, the cat is very nervous and must be coaxed gently and soothingly before any attempt is made to touch it. When the face assumes the alert expression described previously, then it has relaxed. If, however, the ears are held well back and the eyes are narrowed and looking straight at you, the cat is not nervous, just very nasty, and it may well lunge forward at any moment to bite, possibly striking out with its claws at the same time. But when the ears are laid flat to the head, the eyes narrowed to a slit and the cat emits a loud growl, obviously it is in quite a dangerous frame of mind and should be left well alone. Talking to it, though, as long as you are well out of reach, can sometimes cause it to relax, especially if the aggressive posture is caused because it is in strange surroundings. A crouching cat, ears flat to the head and lips drawn back in a growling snarl, is impossible to handle and must be left to settle down, for it will come forward to attack if it is exhibiting this offensive expression.

The tail of the cat is also very expressive, for when held upright with just the extreme tip waving gently to and fro, the cat is in an affable mood. If it is held very stiffly upright, it is inquiring and alert but friendly. If it is fluffed up and upright, it is a little afraid but still prepared to be friends, but if it is fluffed up and tucked between the legs or waving furiously from side to side, beware! A very angry, dominant cat will not even fluff up its tail; it will lash it from side to side just before springing on its enemy, at the same time growling loudly.

Cats also use their voices to communicate, and a whole repertoire of sounds can be distinguished even by the unsophisticated human ear. Communication by sound between cats is very acute, for the structure of the ear, with its forward, alert placement and mobile pinna, can help fix sound sources very accurately, obviously an asset to a seminocturnal animal, liking to hunt at night in the wild. Sharp, high-pitched sound at a certain level has been found to stimulate defecation in young cats; obviously, this is the sound emitted by the mother at weaning when encouraging her kittens in toilet training. The same sound has been found to act as a sexual stimulant in adult cats. Soft, rustling sounds are very exciting to all cats, and obviously closely approximate the sounds of prey. To enrich the environment of young kittens, cellophane crushed up and allowed to unwrinkle itself produces a similar, exciting effect, and the rustling of dried straws is also effective.

Cats purr when content by a mechanism not fully understood. They also purr when in great pain in the terminal stages of severe illness, a fact which has comforted scores of pet owners, who are able to claim that their pet purred as it died. Cats first learn to purr as nursing kittens, then learn to repeat this when pleasurably handled by humans. They often purr while apparently sleeping, and purring does seem to be contagious; if one of a group of cats starts, the whole lot will shortly be purring happily in unison.

The queen has a whole range of sounds she uses to communicate with her kittens, from the low, soft "prrrrp" which causes them to lift their heads and go to her, to the deep "MMMraow" that she makes when bringing them some prey or a morsel of food to encourage them to start with solids. If a kitten is missing, she emits a very loud, high-pitched "M-OW-Www," trailing off on a plaintive note.

The language of love in cats is also very varied and goes through a whole range of sound. The male makes encouraging "prrping" noises while courting the female. Her precoitive calls are loud, sometimes plaintive, high-pitched wails, sometimes deep, moaning, growl-like cries. Her screams on penetration are like the cries of a banshee, and during the recovery periods, she makes cross, scolding, little growling cries.

Cats make sounds which their owners soon learn to understand, from the general-alert call to be let either in or out of the door, to the coaxing mew when they think they should have their breakfast before anyone else gets theirs. The cry of a cat in distress carries far and wide, but is usually emitted only when the animal first becomes caught up, trapped or finds itself confined in a strange place, a fact which makes it difficult sometimes to find a lost or injured cat. Cats rarely cry with pain, except at the first shock, and accept injury with withdrawn fortitude. Queens sometimes cry out in labor, a groaning expulsion of breath which seems to ease the muscle spasms, but often purr their way through the long process of birth.

Some cats even appear to "talk" to their owners. Siamese in particular are always extremely vocal, and have clear, strong voices. Many, if addressed in a serious, non-bantering way, will deign to answer, using several tonal expressions and series of notes. Other Foreign breeds often make conversation with their owners, and most cats, if encouraged to do so, will mew in response to the calling of their names.

CHAPTER

10

Sexual Behavior in the Cat

Although some cats breed only in the spring, it is true to say that the species does not have set seasons of the year for estrus. The Foreign short-haired breeds, in particular, are highly reproductive and would have three or four litters each year if allowed to do so. Weather seems to play a part in the breeding cycles of most cats if they are allowed the freedom of the garden for exercise, or live in outdoor catteries, but queens kept in centrally heated conditions will breed at any season of the year. Farm cats usually have a litter in late February or early March and another in June or July, and, if the autumn is mild, yet another litter may be born in September or October.

Sexual maturity is attained at varying ages in both males and females. Male cats can be potent at anywhere from six to eighteen months of age, and it has been known for a female kitten to show signs of estrus at sixteen weeks, while others have remained quiet and tranquil until nearly two years of age. On the whole, the Siamese and Foreign breeds seem to develop earlier than the British and Persian cats. Most females seem to come into season for the first time in the January or February of the first year after their birth, and as any owner of pedigreed stud males will confirm, a mild, sunny spell of weather following a long period of cold and damp will bring a spate of telephone calls from desperate owners wanting to mate frantically calling queens.

Both male and female cats continue to breed throughout their entire life spans, but the prime years of fertility are ages two to seven for the male cat and about two to eight for the female. Sexual and physical maturity do not always coincide in cats. A female attaining puberty very young should be restrained from mating, for she may not have the strength to feed and rear the resulting litter. Unless constant calling endangers the health of the young queen, she should be mated at about ten months of age so that she has attained the age of one year by the time the kittens are born after their sixty-five-day gestation period. If she remains quiet until well over a year of age, so much the better.

The formation of the kittens in embryo takes a toll of

the calcium reserves of the queen, and this substance must be replaced in the diet, or behavioral effects may be observed. A queen lacking calcium at the time of birth may attack and kill the newborn kittens. The lack of calcium affects pathways in the brain which allow the secretion of the hormones which stimulate milk flow and the mother instinct. Lactating also depletes bodily reserves of the vital calcium. Whereas the cat in the wild, by eating every scrap of her prey including the calcium-rich skeleton, would get plenty of replacement of this essential mineral, domesticated cats, fed on muscle meat alone, often show a serious deficiency. Queens allowed to breed too frequently may not have time, between litters, to replace the lost calcium within their own skeletal framework and may then suffer from lactational tetany while feeding a litter, go into shock and die.

The signs of estrus in the female cat are quite easy to recognize. First comes the proestrus period during which the uterus and vagina undergo subtle changes in preparation for mating and possible pregnancy. The vulva swells very slightly and the behavior changes, the cat becoming rather restless, pacing the house and being extra-affectionate when handled. The second stage, three to five days after the onset of the first stage, is the estrus period proper, which lasts about one week. This is the period during which mating will take place. The queen becomes more restless and rolls on the floor. She cries a lot and will look agitatedly from the window, escaping from the house if at all possible. As this period reaches its peak, the rolls become violent and ecstatic, the cries more urgent, and with a deeper tone. From time to time the mating position will be adopted, and if the back of the animal is touched, she will tread with the hind legs, holding her tail to one side. If mating does not take place, eventually and to the owner's great relief, a third stage called metestrus occurs. No ovulation having occurred, the reproductive organs quiet down and enter the period known as anestrus, the resting stage, before the next cycle begins.

Male cats do not have periods of heat and are capable of coition at any time after they attain sexual maturity, although after a long illness or a busy stud season, the libido may be lowered a little. The call of the queen in season, and the smell she emits, both serve to excite the stud male even if she is out of sight. The higher notes, inaudible to human ears, are thought to be particularly attractive and exciting to the male cat. The queen's posturing and rolling he finds quite irresistible.

In controlled matings of pedigreed cats, the owner of the queen contacts the owner of the selected male when the first signs of estrus are apparent. On the second or third day of the proper estrus period, when the queen adopts the mating position when stroked, she is taken or sent to the stud. Male cats at public stud are housed in spacious outdoor accommodations, with an airy building complete with a special pen for the visiting queen, and a large exercise run. The queen is placed in the special pen, for, although eager to mate, she will play hard to get until used to the smell of the strange male, and she may well bite and scratch him.

In the pen the queen will roll and posture, emitting deep, crooning sounds. The stud cat then becomes very interested, sitting and watching her, ears and whiskers pointing forward, and he will make deep crooning noises back to her. The male makes small forward movements toward the queen, sitting, often with one paw upraised, until only the wire separates the two cats. When the queen shows that she is ready for mating and exhibits no inclination to hiss at the male, the partition is removed and the cats are allowed to mate.

First, the male runs at the queen from the side and rear while she crouches, head down, hindquarters raised and tail bent to the side. He grasps the loose skin at the back of her neck firmly in his jaws and places one foreleg on either side of her body. With his hind legs, the male then gently treads at the back of the queen, encouraging her to lift her hindquarters even more.

When the queen relaxes, the male arches his back around the body of the queen, and penetration takes place, upon which the queen emits a loud, screaming cry. The experienced male holds tightly to her scruff while he thrusts forward a few times and ejaculates. Then he releases the queen and leaps well away. As soon as she is freed, the queen snarls, hisses and turns to strike out at the male, then she rolls vigorously along the floor, often growling and hissing, before washing the vaginal area. The male will also be cleaning his genital area, usually from a high stool or other safe vantage point where he can keep a wary eye on the queen at this unpredictable stage in the proceedings. A few minutes later, both cats will be ready and eager to mate again, and this will continue, if not checked, through the whole estrus period.

Free mating of cats is rather different, for the odor and calling of the queen will have attracted several ready and willing males into the vicinity. The queen will be courted and much caterwauling will be heard as the males square up to one another, each trying to assert his superiority for the privilege of being the first to mate with the queen. Silent and very bitter, bloody battles break out among the males, often resulting in two exhausted combatants, while the queen appears to revel in the attention, rolling, twisting and posing, until she is eventually mounted by the dominant male. She will roll and cry after mating, and then be mounted again by the same male, or the next in order of dominance, being mated many times by several males during the next day or so.

Male cats are motivated by their sexual urges most of the time if given their liberty. The entire tom is not a pleasant house pet. As far as he is concerned, his owners merely offer food and lodgings between amorous forays. The tom fights many fierce battles and receives many battle scars. The long canine teeth of cats inflict deep wounds which heal on the skin surface while the bacteria injected into the tissue below multiply and form abscesses. Tomcats fight vigorously and in short, sharp bursts. Two toms will square up to each other by walking stiff-legged and with tail erect around each other, perhaps sniffing at the area one has just sprayed on or rubbed against. Occasionally, if no female is present, nose touching or sniffing at the other's anus may occur.

During the squaring-up procedure, the male cats puff out their already naturally thickened jowls and hunch their shoulders. The fur on the back and tail fluffs up, each hair becoming erect and causing the animal to look much larger and more frightening to its opponent. They turn sideways, presenting the largest possible area to their adversary. Much growling, muffled and under the breath, goes on, plus some lip-smacking, salivating behavior, usually in the more nervous and inexperienced of the two.

When a fight occurs, the males bite and lunge for the other's neck and throat region. They roll over and over and rake at each other's bodies with their hind legs, tearing out great lumps of fur, then break, and one may attempt to dash away. The other will then bite at the tail-root region. Many toms have to be treated for four abscesses around the tail and testes where the four canine teeth have penetrated.

Male cats do not always fight on meeting, and a dominant male will assert his seniority by biting the scruff of a submissive male, mounting him, then letting go and walking away. A male cat that does not want to fight will either avoid a dominant male, or crouch, mew and present the scruff. Few cats indulge in homosexual behavior; the mounting by the dominant male is merely to assert his dominance.

It is extremely rare for a male cat to fight a female, although confined, possibly frustrated male stud cats have been known to attack and, in very rare cases, even kill a queen in estrus, after the queen has turned, naturally, on him after mating. Female cats, though, will quite often fight, but this is usually through jealousy, either over food, over kittens or for the owner's affections, and a queen will fight a marauding tom to the death, if necessary, to protect her nursing litter.

CHAPTER

11

Maternal Behavior

The female cat is a model mother, keeping her babies well nourished, clean and contented from the moment they are born until they are ready to face the world alone and fend for themselves. From the time of puberty, the female cat is geared to motherhood, maturing early and being persistent in her efforts to meet a suitable mate. The male cat takes no part in the rearing of the litter, his job being solely to fertilize the queen. Female cats are spontaneous ovulators; that is, they shed the ripe eggs after being stimulated by the act of mating. Persistent calling in estrus when the queen is confined and not allowed to mate can eventually cause her to become sterile, through not having shed any ova.

From the moment of conception, the queen's body prepares for the birth of her kittens. The hormones secreted by the glands give rise to certain behavior patterns. She becomes more constantly alert in order to protect her unborn litter from danger. She eats well and selectively, with a good appetite, and takes lots of careful exercise. She eats the tips of choice grasses and hunts with a sense of purpose and enjoyment. Her grooming sessions are meticulously carried out, and she always sleeps in a concealed or high place.

Toward the end of her pregnancy, she will jump and move more cautiously. She grooms her enlarging breasts frequently and very carefully, but she may be unable to reach her anal area at this time. Every possible nesting site will be explored, and a good owner will provide a suitable box with a large pile of clean newspaper inside, so that the queen can shred these and make a perfect kittening bed.

At this time, the queen will try several places before deciding that the box provided is perfect. She may tear up garments, dressmaking patterns or precious books or papers if these are left in half-open drawers into which she can crawl. She tears material by holding it with her paws and pulling it with her teeth. Newspapers are torn into very tiny shreds by the queen, reducing a hard pile to a soft, downy heap.

Just prior to the birth, the queen becomes restless and may pay several visits to her litter box without performing, looking behind her in a slightly puzzled way. Eventually, she will go to her box and start her labor. Most queens have their kittens without any problems, and these may be presented head first or tail first: breech births seem to be as common as head presentations and do not cause many problems in the cat. At first, a sac of fluid is expelled which dilates the birth passages and the queen licks this away, clearing up the expelled fluids. When the first kitten is born, she licks away the sac membranes and fluid, and vigorously massages life into the tiny creature with her rough tongue. The placenta then emerges, and this is eaten by the queen, who eats along the cord until she reaches a point about an inch from the kitten's body. The rest of the kittens follow and are usually dealt with in the same way.

After the birth of the final kitten, the queen cleans her flanks and hind regions. She then gathers the kittens under her before curling her body around on its side, encircling the litter. She licks them firmly, encouraging them to seek her nipples, and then, purring, relaxes and rests.

Hunting and prey-eating behavior are suppressed at the time of birth in the mother cat, and this is why it is common for cats which have just kittened to accept other small creatures for fostering. Even rats, mice and squirrels, which would normally be quickly killed by the cat, are accepted and cared for while she is in this state. Eating the enriched placenta would probably provide a queen in the wild with enough nourishment to enable her to remain in the nest recovering her strength for at least twenty-four hours. Certainly, queens which eat the placenta have a better milk supply than those which, through domestication, seem to be at a loss during the birth process.

The queen does not leave her litter alone for very long, merely leaving the nest to relieve herself and to feed. She stimulates urination and defecation in the kittens by licking them after they have nursed, and she swallows the excreted matter, thus keeping the nest spotlessly clean. When the kittens reach the age of about three weeks, most queens decide to move them to another site, and will go to great lengths in order to satisfy this very pressing urge. Each kitten is grasped right around its neck in the queen's jaws, then, by flexing her neck and holding her head high, she carries it firmly and gently, keeping her forelegs straddled so as not to bump it. One by one the kittens are taken to the new nest. When picked up in this manner, the kitten immediately goes completely limp and remains quiet until put down again.

Queens give their kittens virtually undivided attention until they are about four weeks old, then they spend less time with them. Most will bring small morsels of food to the litter and encourage them to eat, and will also try to show the kittens where to go for toilet purposes. A whole range of language is used by the queen at this stage in her litter's development, and she plays games with them, helping to develop reflex actions and hunting behavior through play. The queen calls the kittens to follow her when she makes short excursions outside, but if any show signs of distress, she quickly lifts them in her jaws and takes them back to the nest box. Should the kittens be extra noisy or torment her too much by biting her neck or tail, she will subdue them with a firm paw, and may even aim a well-directed slap at a particularly naughty kitten. Now and again, she will roll over when the kittens attempt to nurse, hold them in her forepaws and give short, sharp bites to the neck, at the same time raking gently with her back feet, letting them know that it is time for them to be eating solid food.

Even when the kittens are practically weaned, the queen will still groom them very thoroughly, and they will often lick her about the face and neck in return. Also, she will still be very protective toward the kittens when strangers arrive or if there are any strange noises or smells about. Any unusual sounds will cause the queen to run about the room in an alert and agitated manner, and the kittens take this as an indication to bolt for cover, possibly triggered by the queen's distinctive growling cry.

The depletion in the queen's skeletal calcium reserves at this time causes her to prevent the kittens from nursing, although she is still prepared to wash and protect them. As she licks them, they try to feed, but she prevents this by sitting firmly down, her four feet tucked well in so that the kittens cannot suckle. If they are very persistent, she will jump to some high vantage point where she can watch over them but where they cannot reach her.

Eventually, the kittens are totally independent, and although the queen comes running if any give a distressed call, she is already getting ready for her next family. Her hormones are preparing her body for proestrus, and when the true estrus period arrives, she will be ready and willing to mate again.

Maternal reactions are so strong in the cat that, if a litter dies, estrus will occur almost spontaneously, and the queen will mate and conceive straightaway. Sometimes, though, having lost her kittens, the queen will mother anything in sight; even another adult cat will be approached, grasped by the scruff and pulled firmly toward the nest box. Toys and small, warm woolen objects, such as socks and gloves, may be put in the nest box. Luckily, the hormonal balance soon restores the queen to normality, and unless ill or weak, she may be mated up again when next in estrus.

Hunting, Killing
and Eating

The domestic cat has been referred to as the "tiger in the hearth" and although it can be the most docile, gentle and loving of pets, it has an inborn love of hunting for fun as well as for food. Even a well-fed, pampered cat will occasionally seek out prey for sport, and it is true to say that well-fed farm cats hunt better than those left to their own devices entirely. After years of domestication, the cat shows remarkable powers of detecting, stalking, capturing and dispatching other small animals and birds, frogs and insects, some of which it may eat, and others bring home to present as trophies to its owner.

Predatory behavior patterns appear in the young kitten when the mother first brings small morsels of food to the nest, making her characteristic, exciting call to attract the kittens' attention to the scrap. The mother may pat or toss the food about the nest and encourage the kittens to pounce on it before eating. The kittens practice hunting motions with their littermates, crouching in wait before pouncing upon each other and giving short, sharp bites in the neck region. The mother encourages hunting-style play by waving her tail enticingly, and showing the kittens how to bite and hold.

Given the opportunity, almost any cat will hunt unless allowed to become so obese that the exercise causes distress to the heart or lungs. Usually, the cat prefers to hunt alone, although cases have been known where two or more cats, very fond of each other, have made joint hunting expeditions. Two tabbies, mother and son, were inseparable and would hunt wood pigeons together. The mother would climb the pines and dislodge the torpid, roosting birds, which would drop, to be quickly dispatched by her son below, then both would share the meal.

Usually, cats hunt in their own territory, though some country cats may have a favorite wood or copse they visit from time to time. They prefer to hunt in the early morning or at twilight, and have excellent vision in poor light. Acute hearing helps to pinpoint small animals, and its whiskers, facial hairs and ear tufts all help the cat to move safely and easily through dense undergrowth. When the prey is located accurately, the powerful hind legs propel the cat rapidly forward, the streamlined body aimed at the prey. Extended claws grasp the victim, holding it with the angled "thumb," and the sharp canine teeth kill swiftly with that well-practiced neck bite learned in kittenhood games. If there is no chance of the prey escaping, the cat may indulge in its rather unpleasant habit of teasing its victim before dealing the death blow. It will not do this, though, if there is any chance of the creature's escaping completely. Mother cats often bring back live prey as hunting practice for their kittens.

When hunting birds in fairly open ground, the cat stalks them carefully. First it approaches the birds as quietly and closely as possible, without causing them to take flight, and then flattens its body and head close to the ground. With fluid, almost imperceptible movements, the cat then slides forward, ears, shoulderblades and hips gliding toward the feeding flock. When within striking distance, the cat tensions its hind legs under the body, the tail lashes from side to side, the hips also swing from side to side, energy is built up and is then released as the cat plummets forward, pinning the victim with its forepaws, and dispatching it with the neck bite.

Cats like only freshly killed meat, and if they decide to eat the prey, will usually devour the entrails first. A nursing or pregnant queen will generally eat the whole carcass of a mouse or bird, including the fur or feathers and skeleton, and may regurgitate some of the less digestible portions later. Wildcats probably eat only two or three times per week, gorging themselves at each sitting, then fasting until prompted by hunger to kill again. Because of the high fluid content of fresh prey, cats in the wild state sel-

dom need to drink, whereas domestic cats, fed on an unnatural diet, especially if the food consists of the complete
dried-meat substitutes, must be provided with fresh, clean
drinking water at all times.

Hunting provides more for the cat than a means to satisfy its appetite, as may be confirmed by the many times it
will hunt, kill and present the complete prey to its owner.
The hunting and killing instincts are inborn, and the opportunity to hunt occasionally should not be denied the
country-dwelling cat. The apartment-dwelling cat can
have the sport compensated for to some extent by intelligent thinking on the part of its owner, who can play
teasing games with his cat. Pulling a catnip mouse on a
string around the furniture or hiding it under cushions,
games with feathers or even rolled-up paper balls tossed
around the room for retrieval, all help make up for the loss
of exercise afforded by hunting.

In playing with its prey, the cat often appears to be
practicing its hunting and trapping techniques, and even
after the *coup de grâce* is given, the cat may be seen to be in
a highly aroused state. Such an excited cat will continue to
toss the mouse or bird into the air, spin and dive upon it,
knocking it along the floor by batting it rapidly with alternate feet, diving upon it again and making a series of
rapid neck-bite movements. The dead creature may be
trapped under a low piece of furniture where the cat will
swoop and dive toward it, stretching out the forelegs
under the concealing ledge and fishing out the prey. The
hooking motions used by the cat in fishing may be observed if a small piece of tempting food is placed in a narrow jar, too small for the cat to get its head in.

Eventually, an intelligent cat will reach in with a forepaw and delicately hook out the morsel with its claws.

The teeth of the cat are very specialized, with the canines long and pointed for killing and gripping the prey, and for opening up the abdomen. The sharp, serrated premolars are used for shearing off small portions of flesh which may then be swallowed whole. The cat's jaws do not allow for grinding of food, being hinged in a particular way in the skull, and the cat has few molars. It is important occasionally to feed bones and lumps of meat to the pet cat to keep the teeth, gums and jaws in good condition. A diet consisting solely of soft canned meats is a sure way to ruin the cat's mouth.

A little careful thought about the cat's natural instincts of hunting, killing and eating should help the intelligent owner to compensate for the first two with games, toys and amusements, and to make sure that his pet has a well-balanced and sensible diet, giving plenty of healthful exercise to the mouth and jaws.

What must be remembered when dealing with small kittens, however, is that hunting and killing are practiced from a very early age, and that many household objects which might be considered fair game by the kitten could do it harm. That thread in the eye of a needle stuck into the spool on the side table is quite exciting to a small kitten. It will pat the thread and chew on it, possibly swallowing the end. The rest of the thread will follow down the throat, followed in turn by the needle, now worked free from the spool. Before you know it, you have a frantic kitten with a sewing needle lodged in its throat. Rubber bands dropped carelessly on the floor and forgotten may be patted around and chewed up, causing serious gastric upsets. A dangling electric cord, part of the furniture to a human, becomes an exciting prey substitute to a small kitten, to be pounced upon and bitten into with sharp little teeth. If the cord is plugged into a live socket, the teeth can cause a contact in the wires and the kitten will be electrocuted. Many objects, taken for granted as harmless to ourselves, can prove dangerous, even fatal, to the developing kitten following its inborn instincts of stalking and hunting.

CHAPTER

13

Sleeping and Washing

If one spends any time at all observing feline behavior, it soon becomes apparent that cats spend a great deal of their time sleeping, and that they take care to wash thoroughly after each meal. Cats seem able to sleep at any time of the day or night and in any temperature, although they prefer to find a warm, draft-free spot to take their naps. Even a luxurious cat basket, complete with sheets and blankets, is likely to be ignored in favor of a particular cardboard carton, a high shelf or a favorite chair. The softness or hardness of the sleeping surface seems to be immaterial to sleepy cats, and they have been known to nap on wire-mesh shelving, rough brick walls and on top of a coalbin.

Sleep in the cat has been studied during scientific research into human sleep patterns and behavior, and it has been discovered that cats have two entirely different types of sleep. Catnaps, taken at odd intervals during the day, consist of light sleep, and the blood pressure remains unchanged from that of the waking state. Muscles are slightly tensed and the temperature drops very slightly. Electroencephalograms, known as EEGs, taken of cats during periods of light sleep show characteristic "slow" wave patterns. As the sleep becomes deeper, the cat's blood pressure slowly falls and its temperature rises, the muscle tone relaxes and the EEG begins to show short, sharp wave patterns. In deep, or paradoxical sleep, a defense mechanism comes into play, and the hearing is particularly acute. A sudden noise will alert the cat from deep sleep to immediate wakefulness.

During paradoxical sleep, cats dream. The eyelids twitch over rapidly moving eyes, the cat may purr and mutter, its paws may twitch, and its legs may stir and move as though running or jumping. This type of sleep makes up about a third of the sleeping time of cats, and it is essential that they have the facilities—peace and quietness—to enter this phase, as it is important to their health and well-being. The first week of the newborn kitten's life is spent in almost constant paradoxical sleep. Although it is known that paradoxical sleep is vital to the cat, as it is to humans, and that the dreaming that occurs at this time is also necessary, it is not yet fully understood just why this is so. In experiments in which cats were deprived of this deep sleep for several weeks at a time, it was noticed that their heart rates sped up, and when they were allowed to sleep as and when they wished after the experimental period was up, the animals spent very long periods in deep sleep as if to try to catch up. Only after some time, when the usual pattern of light- and deep-sleep periods had been regained, did the heart rates return to normal, and cats deprived of deep sleep for twenty days took ten days to return to normal.

It is now thought that dreaming occurs when the brain sorts through the events of the day and stores the important parts in the long-term memory store. This would help to explain why the newborn kitten has only deep sleep patterns, going directly from this state to wakefulness and back again, and only at about four weeks of age does it start having periods of light sleep, coinciding with the completion of the wiring system within the brain itself.

Cats vary in the postures that they adopt before settling down to sleep; some prefer to stretch out on their bellies, some on their sides and some tightly curled. The lower the temperature, the tighter they will curl up, head tucked under the tail and the tail curled over the head, all four paws neatly turned in to the belly. Many cats like to sleep with their heads hanging downward, and some place their forepaws over their eyes as if to shut out the light. Kittens need lots of sleep and often just seem to drop off in the middle of an exciting game. They adopt any and every position imaginable but often crawl into an untidy heap, providing each other with extra warmth.

On awakening from sleep, the cat will stretch its body sinuously, flexing every muscle and extending the claws on its forepaws. It may also flex the jaw muscles in a mighty yawn. It is then ready for action. Occasionally, the awakened cat may decide to go through its complicated and very thorough washing routine, especially if it has been sleeping in full sunshine or under an infrared lamp. It seems that the effect of light and warmth on its coat stimulates the washing reflexes into action.

For washing, the cat uses its tongue and paws. The tongue, being covered with little projections called papillae, is rough, and is used to clean the fur most thoroughly. The routine adopted by most cats after eating and on waking follows the usual stretching of the muscles. The cat then sits up and flicks its tongue all around its lips. Licking a paw until quite damp, the cat then uses this to wash its face and head, knuckling into the ears and eyes and down the sides of the nose.

First one side of the head is cleaned, then the other. The tongue is then employed to wash down each shoulder and foreleg, the teeth often coming into play to clear any tangled fur or to remove any substance sticking to the coat or between the toes. Then the flanks are cleaned, the genital area, then down the hind legs and finally the tail.

Some cats wash a great deal, while others seem to attend to matters of hygiene only when really necessary. Most cats will lick and groom themselves after being petted or stroked by strangers, as if to remove the alien smell on the coat. Friendly cats will indulge in social grooming, each attending to the spots that the other cannot reach. Cats enjoy this and will often lick each other's faces after a meal, before settling down to sleep.

Queens wash their kittens from the moment of birth, using the rough tongue in two ways: first, to remove the membranes of the birth sac from the face and head of the kitten, and to lick away traces of amniotic fluid which could be inhaled; and second, to lick the kitten roughly from tail to head, lifting and drying the coat and simultaneously stimulating respiration and circulation. She licks so hard that the kitten is often lifted up slightly, and she will also lick the bedding free from traces of blood and mucus from the birth.

Orphan kittens must have the queen's functions performed by their human foster parents. Not only must they be fed carefully formulated meals, but they also must have the essential licking processes compensated for. Pads of warm, damp cotton are used to wipe all around the orphan's face and mouth, then used fairly firmly on the body area from head to tail. A fresh piece is dampened and squeezed out, then used to wipe the genital area, copying the method employed by the queen, until the kitten has passed urine and feces into the pad. Then the tiny animal can be put in a warm box to sleep.

Sick cats stop washing themselves, and it is up to the owner, acting as nurse, to take over this essential function until health is restored. Many cats, especially those suffering from severe cases of cat flu, die not because of the disease alone but also because they lose the will to live. This will can be put back into the cat by careful and intelligent nursing. The cat with cat flu usually feels very ill indeed, having a fever and congestion of the upper respiratory tract and lungs. The eyes and nose are full of catarrh, the throat ulcerated and sore; the cat just wants to be left alone to die in peace. It cannot see or smell, and its throat is too sore to swallow food comfortably. Having force-fed the cat with nourishing liquid food, the owner must then bathe and clean its caked eyelids and nostrils, applying petroleum jelly to prevent cracking of the delicate tissues. Honey on a small spatula relieves the soreness of the throat; then the animal should be gently brushed and massaged all over the body, the limbs flexed and stretched and the anal regions sponged gently. Well wrapped up in warm blankets, the sick cat should be carried around his favorite spots in the garden. Cats "given up" by the veterinarians have recovered full health after this sort of extra-tender, loving care.

If cats become very dirty, or soiled with toxic substances, they may be bathed, using specially formulated shampoos and comfortably hot water. An old wives' tale states that washing a cat prevents it from ever again attempting to wash itself, but this just is not true. After a good bath and a careful rinsing, the cat should be rubbed as dry as possible with a rough terry towel, then the coat combed gently into place. The first thing the cat will do is to shake its body hard, then delicately shake each paw, and then sit down and quietly and methodically proceed to lick and groom every hair until restored to dryness.

Unusual Behavior

Before we discuss unusual behavior in domestic cats, we should think about what we mean by normal behavior, bearing in mind the natural instincts of the creature in the wild, and the ways in which we have expected it to adapt to life in the home, acceptable to our own standards. The wildcat's life consists of hunting behavior, to provide it with food; sexual behavior to enable reproduction; and self-preservation behavior, for times when the predator becomes, temporarily, the prey.

We provide food for our pet cats, we neuter them to take away the need or desire for reproduction, or, alternatively, we breed them selectively and in far-from-natural conditions, and we protect them from hazards such as extremes of temperature and from anything that might harm or injure them. It seems hardly surprising, therefore, that some cats exhibit strange or abnormal behavior.

Faulty or inadequate diet can induce strange behavior patterns. The brain needs proper nourishment, and all the body cells, constantly renewing themselves, require the metabolism to work normally. Deficiencies of certain vitamins and minerals can cause nervous symptoms to appear, while some nervous disorders may be cured by adding vitamins to the diet under veterinary supervision. A condition resembling epilepsy was found to be caused in cats when fed meat, prepared for dogs, containing the preservative benzoic acid. Dogs are not affected by benzoic acid, but those cats fed food containing this substance became completely wild and hysterical. Some went into convulsions, some developed muscular spasms and appeared to be blind. Most died or had to be humanely killed, and a few lucky ones recovered.

Shock or trauma also can cause behavior disorders in the cat. During wartime, after periods of shelling or gunfire, it was discovered that many cats were so affected by the noise levels that they crawled into dark corners and either died or, when extricated, were found to be past recovery and to need euthanasia. Even unskilled or rough handling, or perhaps painful veterinary treatment without adequate anesthesia, can result in an unbalanced and unpredictable cat, and some cats have had their usual good natures ruined forever by being frightened by rough handling at cat shows.

Severe shock may follow a fight with another cat or dog, or a narrow escape from injury in a road accident. The symptoms are depression and listlessness, loss of appetite, a high pulse rate and dampness of the pads of the feet. The cat may want to hide, it may shiver, the pupils may dilate and it may be hypersensitive to touch. The only treatment for such severe shock is to pick the cat up carefully, using a towel or blanket to avoid being bitten or scratched, then place it in a safe carrier in a warm, dark place with complete quietness until it has fully recovered. Veterinary treatment with tranquilizers may be required in such cases; quite often, cats develop phobias following such experiences.

Shock reactions can result in collapse and very sudden death in highly strung cats, especially those which have been overhumanized. Sometimes, in cases of restraint for veterinary examination or injection, the overstimulation of the nervous system brings about a vasovagal attack. It is sad indeed that we should raise pets to be so sensitive that such innocuous handling could distress them so severely as to cause their death. Luckily, this state of affairs occurs only very rarely.

Also very rare, but well documented, is that state of sham death shown by some cats when they are extremely alarmed or surprised by an enemy. The cat assumes a catatonic state known as "playing possum" and looks as though it has dropped down dead. It is not fully understood how this behavior is instigated, but it probably helps to inhibit the chase response in some larger animals and acts as a protection mechanism.

Cats moved to new homes often show disturbed behavior patterns, and the introduction of a new kitten, a new baby or even a new spouse can cause a normally happy, well-balanced pet to become extremely antisocial. Upset routines manifest themselves in a cat's behavior in several ways. The most usual is the breakdown of normal hygiene habits. The cat may urinate or even defecate in places hitherto unthought of, such as the burner of the stove, the center of the quilt in the best bedroom or on soft cushions or rugs. Scolding seems to make matters worse, and the only solution is to confine the cat to an unspoilable room until it has recovered its manners. Cats feeling that their territory has been violated in some way may start to spray the furniture, strop fiercely at the furnishings or deliberately knock down ornaments and books from high shelves. They may go on hunger strikes or even indulge in such behavior as self-mutilation—licking at paws and flanks until they are raw and bleeding. Fur pulling on flanks and chest is also quite common. A Siamese, feeling displaced by his owner's new baby, chewed his tail until three joints were so mutilated that they finally had to be amputated.

Excessive grooming may also be caused by extreme boredom, and cats confined for long periods in badly designed boarding catteries, isolated and without anything to amuse them, may lick areas of skin quite raw. Others may indulge in self-sucking if understimulated, and may suck at paws, flanks, tails or even their own rear nipples. While sucking in this way they may purr, and tread with the forepaws, regressing to early kittenhood. Related to this behavior is the wool-eating syndrome found in some cats, mostly, it would seem, in the Siamese varieties. Possibly an inherited trait, for it does run in families, it is most annoying and difficult to treat. Wool-eaters only have to get into a relaxed state; their eyes glaze slightly and they start to tread and knead with the forepaws, first licking at the woolen object, then tugging at the fabric, sucking and chewing. Some afflicted cats will chew on cottons or other fabrics, but most seem to prefer pure wool. Extensive damage may be done by such cats. Treatment with vitamin supplements, minerals and a change of diet has worked in some cases but not in others.

It is rare for a pet cat to become aggressive and unmanageable unless it is reacting to extreme fear at being cornered or at being cruelly teased. Bad or unkind handling at some stage in its development may have caused unpleasant associations for the animal, or there may be some strange noise or smell with which it associates danger, and which makes it dangerous to handle at a particular moment. A cat being menaced by a dog will bite the owner if he picks it up out of harm's way. A kitten, terrified of the noise of the vacuum cleaner, will leap high into the air, or bite and scratch if touched by a human hand. This behavior, though unusual, is quite normal and part of the cat's defense mechanism.

Although cats are notorious for their dislike of water, some seem to revel in playing with dripping faucets, others like to roll in the damp bathtub and a few enjoy swimming. Cats are adept at fishing, and usually fish by wading into the shallows and hooking out small fish with a deft movement of the forepaw, claws unsheathed and hooked. Some cats are intrigued by snow and ice and will bound about in such conditions, pushing their muzzles under the snow and rolling in ecstasy. The effect is probably the same as in rolling on cool concrete. When let out into the garden, most cats will immediately seek a paved area or path, and roll, pushing their backs hard against the cold, hard surface before sitting up to have a good, thorough wash.

Much unusual behavior in the domestic cat is brought about by disease or by the administration of certain drugs, which affect or destroy vital centers in the brain. The behavior patterns may be temporarily upset, but may recover with care, good diet and perhaps some medication, although in some cases the damage may be irreparable and the behavior patterns then permanently impaired. Damage to certain parts of the brain may cause deafness. Some cats are born deaf due to a congenital defect, and this disability needs particular care, for a deaf animal is easily startled, suddenly seeing something but not having heard its approach. Some deaf cats have certain parts of the hearing mechanism—those which cope with vibration—still intact. It is then possible to communicate with them, after experimentation, by banging certain objects which cause vibrations which the animals can pick up. Deaf cats are particularly vulnerable to road accidents and should be carefully watched over at all times.

Sexual aggressions and disorders occasionally show themselves in pet cats. Young males often become difficult to handle if kept entire and confined. When they are castrated, their dispositions improve. Unspayed females, deprived of motherhood, call constantly and can become so frustrated that they start mothering toys, begin self-sucking or become dirty in their habits, often spraying the furnishings. Unless breeding is the aim, it would seem advisable to neuter both males and females at about six months of age if they are to be happy, well-balanced pets.

Odd behavior, as opposed to unusual behavior, is apparent in the cat if it is carefully watched throughout a normal day. If it is scolded, it will go and sit with its back to its owner and look into space, ignoring all coaxing calls. If given food of which it is not overfond, it will make rude, covering-up gestures with its forepaws around the plate, as if to cover, with earth, something quite unmentionable. If it is shut indoors, it may paw monotonously at the windowpane with alternate paws, as though, with concerted effort, it might manage to burrow through.

On the whole, considering the ways in which we expect the cat to fit in with our own very unnatural ways of life, it remains a very well-balanced, well-adjusted creature, and perhaps this is why it suits us so well as a pet, for what could be more relaxing at the end of a hard day than to sit comfortably in a favorite chair with a calm, serene and beautiful cat upon our knees?

The Character and Language
of the Cat

"The Cat—though an animal of prey—is a useful domestic. It is neither wanting in sagacity nor sentiment, but its
attachments are stronger to places than to persons. The
form of its body corresponds with its disposition. The cat
is handsome, light, adroit and cleanly, and voluptuous; he
loves ease and searches out the softest furniture in order to
repose on and rest himself. . . . Young cats are gay,
lively, pretty and would be very proper to amuse children,
if the strokes of their paws were not to be feared. Their

disposition, which is an enemy to all restraint, renders them capable of a regular education.

"Cats seem to have a natural dread of water, cold and bad smells. They are very fond of perfumes, and gladly suffer themselves to be taken and caressed by persons who use them. . . . Their eyes shine in the dark, almost like diamonds and reflect outwardly, during the night, the light which they may be said to have imbibed during the day."

The above was written by the eminent naturalist M. de Buffon, as long ago as the late eighteenth century. Although many will not agree with all that he says, much of it is true, except the reference to the eyes shining in the dark, which is now known to be due to reflection of light.

What is it about cats that makes them so much admired by many people, yet so disliked by others? A number of people visiting a cat show were questioned at random about their attitude toward cats. They had quite definite feelings, but the answers differed considerably. In fact, some of the answers made one wonder what the people were doing at a cat show!

Cats were liked for their aloofness, their companionship, their cuddliness, their character, their intelligence and so on. They were disliked for the way that they stared at people, making them feel uncomfortable; their cruelty to mice and birds; and their bad tempers. All who owned cats said theirs was more intelligent than any other, and many cats seemed to have individual tricks which endeared them even more to their owners. Men, in particular, were very proud of their own cats although often they disliked those belonging to other people.

Some people are ailurophobes, that is, cat haters. Many cannot bear to be in a room with a cat and can sense if there is one in the house even if they are unable to see it, often feeling quite faint. Napoleon was one such person, and, it is believed, Hitler, another.

As we have seen, there are definite differences among the characters of the main pedigreed varieties: the long-haired, the short-haired British, the Siamese and the other Foreign short-hairs. But people who have known many cats and their owners over the years have realized that it is the interest and affection shown to a cat that will influence its personality more than the particular breed or variety.

All cats are individualists. It is no use thinking all Siamese are alike in character or that all long-haired kittens are quiet and placid. That is the whole charm of cats: they are unpredictable, they have diverse personalities and characters, and dislike being dictated to. There is nothing submissive about them. They like to do things when they please and if they please, and not because they are forced to. One can *claim* to own a cat, but it is very much the other way about. It takes many years of living with cats really to appreciate their good qualities.

One of the qualities not always appreciated nowadays is that cats are natural hunters, and it should be remembered that it was for their prowess in catching mice and rats that they were first esteemed by the early Egyptians. Although there are now many rodent officers and pest controllers, cats are still most useful to farmers in keeping down vermin. Unfortunately, cats are also bird-catchers, although the long-hairs are not as bad in that way as are some of the short-hairs. One disliked trait is the habit of bringing in many of their catches for their owners' approval, such as rats at breakfast time!

Cats will display affection wholeheartedly, putting paws around their owners' necks, even kissing if allowed to do so. It is said that it is all "cupboard love," but many will disagree. Cats appreciate the companionship of humans above everything else and that is probably one of the reasons why they have been so often the pets of artists, writers and poets who spend many hours quietly working. Many cats are miserable if left alone for long hours, moping and losing interest in things.

Cats have been known to make very strange friendships, attaching themselves to horses, goats, rabbits, even elephants. If brought up together, or introduced carefully later, a cat and a dog can live together most happily, and will sleep curled up in the same basket. Siamese, in particular, love the company of another cat, but the long-hairs, although accepting other cats, are not always quite so close to one another.

Cats can be very jealous and can resent attention paid to others, often trying to attract notice to themselves by patting and pawing and twining around their owners' legs. They are possessive about particular chairs and playthings. They can be very observant, noticing changes, and a new piece of furniture will be inspected thoroughly.

They appear to be able to tell the time and, if fed at regular hours, will appear promptly at mealtimes. Many wake up their owners at the same time each morning by biting their ears or patting their faces, and will wait by the gate for the return of the owners if at a set time each day.

Many cats are vain and love admiration, closing their eyes with pleasure, purring when given attention. They have many expressions, being able to show disgust, anger, contempt, terror, boredom, pleasure and a "We are not amused" face when laughed at, which most hate.

To many, the cat is a dumb animal, but this is far from being the case, as, in reality, it is the most vociferous of all animals and the most able to communicate its moods and feelings in a number of sounds and ways. The cat is capable of expressing its sentiments by means of facial expressions, movements of the tail and paws, licking and various sounds produced by the vocal cords.

According to Charles Darwin in his *Expression of Emotions,* "Cats use their voices as a means of expression, and they utter under various emotions and desires at least six or seven different sounds." Anyone who has lived close to a cat for any length of time will no doubt argue that they are capable of a far greater number of sounds than this. In fact, Carl Van Vechten, in *Tiger in the House,* said that Champfleury, the nineteenth-century French writer on cats, "counted sixty-three notes in the mewing of cats, although he admitted that it took an accurate ear and a great deal of practice to distinguish them. On the other hand . . . the Abbe Galiani could only discern twenty notes in the most elaborate mewing." Van Vechten comments: "Anyone who has lived on amicable terms with a cat will have no difficulty in understanding so much of her language; an interested observer may pick up much more."

Comparing cats and dogs and their powers of communication, several writers state that the dog uses vowel sounds only, while the cat uses consonants as well, although they disagree as to the actual ones used. Owners of a number of cats have found that the vocabulary varies greatly from one cat to another, and that some converse much more than others. Most are very polite, answering graciously when spoken to, but one has to live very close to a cat to understand its individual vocabulary.

Cats are affected by the weather. Indeed, it is said that they can be quite good forecasters. A change in ·the weather is generally indicated when the cat starts to dash around the house, while washing behind its ears is taken as a sign of rain. Chasing its tail is also said to foretell change in the weather, while sitting with its back to the fire is said to mean frosty weather. Falling leaves in the autumn are considered playthings, and cats are intrigued by falling snow and seem to love walking in it. Hot sunshine is much appreciated, and frequently a cat will be seen flat on its back, with paws in the air, enjoying a sunbath. Strong winds are viewed with distrust, as cats appear to dislike the feeling of the fur being blown about.

Many love the scent of flowers and will sniff at lavender and sweet-smelling flowers with appreciation.

They will pretend to make out they are in distress just to get attention. Charles Ross, in his *Book of Cats,* written in 1867, tells of a cat that hurt a leg and, while ill, was given milk as a special treat, managing to limp painfully toward the saucer. This went on for some weeks until the leg had healed. The milk was then stopped. After a day or so, the cat started to limp toward its owner, dragging the leg in the hope that it would be given milk.

As cats prefer to do things when they please and are not

very predictable, there have been few performing cats, but there are one or two that have been trained to appear in films, on the stage and on television.

Although cats are photogenic, temperament is very important if a cat is to be a successful "star." There must be strong affection for, and complete trust in the owner. Patience and time will be needed, and simple tricks, such as climbing and jumping off a ladder, will have to be repeated many times, and with a reward being given each time, until the cat realizes what is required and does it to order. The cat must not mind traveling around, going to studios or being handled by strangers. Some cats are natural actors, loving the special attention and playing up to an audience. One well-known television cat model, appearing at a cat show as a special attraction, resented quite openly the fact that another well-known cat personality in the next pen was receiving more admiration, and sat with his head turned disdainfully away.

A cat can be very jealous of another cat in the same household, particularly if it feels the other one is getting more attention, and will push in when it is being stroked and also insist on sitting on the owner's lap at the same time as the other.

As cats have a very keen sense of hearing, well above the human range, they are able to distinguish the sound of one car from another, recognizing the owner's engine noise from that of a visitor's. When they are hunting, they freeze instantly at any rustlings they hear in long grass. A few white cats, particularly those with blue eyes, are born deaf, but animals affected in this way often appear to be especially intelligent and observant, seemingly being able to read their owner's thoughts. They respond to manual signs once they understand their meaning, and will also react quickly to vibrations. A deaf cat should be handled frequently and fussed over, as the human touch is even more appreciated. If one lives in town, the danger is traffic, and it is advisable to have a garden with a high fence, if possible, rather than to let a deaf cat roam freely. If there is no garden, toilet facilities should be provided indoors and the animal exercised on a lead or not allowed out.

Cats are sensual creatures, loving to be stroked and caressed, under the chin and the top of the head being favored spots. Inquisitive and demanding by nature, noisy at times, very quiet at others, they seem to sense sadness and will often comfort their owners in times of distress.

The complex character of the cat is illustrated well by the following quotation from *The Siamese Cat,* written by Sidney and Helen Denham. Although it refers to a Siamese, it is just as true of all cats:

> The ingredients the Creator chose to mix when He decided to make the first Siamese have been given as the grace of the panther, the intelligence of the elephant, the affection of the lovebird, the beauty of the fawn, the softness of down and the swiftness of light.

CHAPTER
16

Behavior of the Pet Cat

It is easy to generalize about the behavior of cats, but really to know and understand a particular animal, the owner should be close to it from kittenhood, watching its development and growth of character. Most kittens have a very short relationship with the mother, so many traits are inherited or instinctive, and early training is essential to correct any would-be unpleasant habits such as the sharpening of claws on the furniture. As touch is very important to a cat, grooming should be started right away, as it not only keeps the fur clean, removing any loose hairs and fleas, but also gets a kitten used to being handled.

It has been realized only comparatively recently that the move to a new home may have a traumatic effect on some kittens, so much so that they become quite ill but not from any specific illness. Missing the companionship of its mother and the rest of the litter, a kitten will sometimes become listless, taking very little interest in food, and will rapidly lose weight, almost fading away. Felines have a very highly strung nervous system and quickly react to changed circumstances. It is, therefore, necessary after obtaining a new kitten to spend as much time with it as possible, and to talk to it constantly so that it will soon react to the human voice and understand a few simple words, get to know its name and come when called.

It is wise for the first few days, at least, to keep closely to the diet sheet which the breeder can supply.

Playtime is an essential part of training: throwing a small ball made of paper or wool and trailing a string will provide exercise and prevent boredom. A kitten will soon learn to retrieve the small ball and will bring it back to the owner time and time again. Dogs can be trained to obey words of command, but cats (and kittens) refuse to be dominated and object most strongly to being forced to do anything against their wills. They are highly intelligent and very quick in thinking.

The majority of kittens are quickly housebroken and will use the litter box or garden, if allowed out there, with no fuss at all. Unfortunately, there are the few that do misbehave. If a kitten does make a mistake, do not rub its nose in it or shout at it. Above all, do not smack it, for this or for any other wrongdoing. It will not realize that it is being punished, but will simply think that it is being hurt and will retaliate. A firm "no" is most effective.

If a kitten persists in being dirty, using the same spot, the place should be washed with a strong-smelling disinfectant. This destroys the smell and should stop the kitten from using it again. A little pepper sprinkled there may also act as a deterrent. It may help if, after sleeping or feeding, the cat is encouraged to use the litter box or the garden. Most cats are naturally clean creatures and will not use a dirty or smelly litter box, so the box should be changed frequently to keep it sweet smelling. There are a number of cat toilet litters on the market which contain a deodorant, keeping down the smell. Remember that if torn-up newspaper is used in the box, the kitten may think that any newspaper left around may be used for the same purpose. If using earth instead of a litter, change it when wet, otherwise there will be a trail of muddy paws throughout the house. It is a good idea to stand the box on a piece of plastic or something similar, to prevent the litter from being scattered. Do not give a young kitten a very high box or bowl to struggle in or out of, as it may hurt itself in doing so and not use it again for that reason.

As mentioned before, the kitten must be trained at an early age not to scratch the furniture or curtains. If the kitten is not allowed into a garden where it can be shown how to use a tree or bush, a scratching post, made for this purpose, may be bought at a pet shop. A large bough, string wound around the kitchen table leg or a piece of carpet nailed to a board may serve the same purpose. If the kitten should attempt to scratch the furniture, say "no" firmly and take it to a place where scratching is permitted.

Kittens can be trained to walk on a lead, the short-haired varieties seeming to adapt more easily to this than the long-haired. A collar on a long-haired kitten to be exhibited at a show may spoil the ruff. The correct collar or harness must be chosen. Small elastic collars, suitable for kittens, may be bought from animal welfare societies or pet shops. The one chosen must be light in weight, as the kitten must be able to free itself should the collar catch on anything.

The time it takes to train a kitten to walk on a lead depends very much on its intelligence and the patience of the owner. The kitten should be allowed to get used to the feel of the collar around its neck for a short period, a day or two, before the lead is attached. At first, some kittens will sit down and refuse to budge, while others dash madly around in all directions. To begin with, a few minutes are sufficient, the time and the length of the walk being increased gradually until the kitten walks quite naturally ahead of you. Eventually, the cat may get quite excited when it sees its collar and lead, knowing what will follow, and obviously looking forward to the outing.

Most kittens learn very quickly and before long may be able to do a few simple tricks; but tricks that are amusing and probably delightful to watch when performed by a young kitten may not be so funny in a cat. Climbing up and sitting on the owner's shoulder may be a charming trick, but a large, hefty cat doing the same trick, often unexpectedly, can be most disconcerting. Jumping onto the table and lapping milk from a jug is a bad habit, and while perhaps a fond owner may not object, visitors to the house may. A small kitten running up the curtains may do no harm, but a heavy cat can do a great deal of damage.

Many cats teach themselves to beg for their food, sitting up gracefully, waving their paws around. Some cats do not lick from saucers at all but use their paws as spoons, dipping in and taking the feed up to their mouths that way.

As the kitten grows into a cat, it will become used to a simple routine, expecting to be fed at certain times and will usually be there, ready and waiting. If a cat is allowed complete freedom, it may decide it does not want to come in when you think it should. One cat will come when you whistle, another will rush in when a bottle of yeast tablets is rattled. One will react to the sound of the shaking of a packet of cornflakes, while yet another will dash in when it hears the chopping up of its raw meat. You may walk around the garden with the cat following you, but the moment you want to pick it up and take it in, it will sense what you are about to do and keep just that distance away from you.

In most writings, the independence of the cat is always stressed and this is true in many ways. A cat does like to do things when it wants to, such as being caressed when it feels like it. On the other hand, it is very much a creature of habit. Most cats have a sense of time and will regularly turn up at the correct hour for feeding, and will make nuisances of themselves if for any reason the meal is late.

A cat that is to be kept purely as a pet should always be neutered. An entire male not kept as a stud may cause problems to his owner. The cat may become aggressive, very restless and dirty about the house. Many owners fear that neutering will change a cat's character, but this rarely happens, although a young male's behavior will certainly alter. If it is not to be used for breeding, a female kitten should be neutered, or spayed as it is called, as otherwise the owner may also face some difficulty with her. There are some female cats that are "silent callers," and the owner may not even be aware that she has been in season, thinking she is just putting on weight, and is most surprised when she produces a family.

As seen in Chapter 10, the majority of females show some signs of coming into season or "in heat." Should any of these signs be apparent, care must be taken by the owner to keep the cat under close supervision. Some females make the most determined efforts to get out, and doors must be kept tightly shut, or she will escape and meet up with the usual ever-hopeful tom, invariably hanging around awaiting his opportunity.

Should this happen, and the cat is pedigreed, it will in no way spoil her for future breeding, as is frequently supposed. It is possible for an injection to be given by a veterinarian within twenty-four hours of the mating to prevent conception, but most breeders are not in favor of this because it has been found that sometimes the cat may have trouble when she has kittens at some future date.

It is not always realized that, even if the female is mated, she may continue to be in season for several days afterward. Indeed, it is possible for dual matings to occur, with the kittens in the same litter having two fathers. If the female is sent away to stud and then allowed out, there may be both mongrel and pedigreed kittens. It is, therefore, only common sense to keep her in close confinement for at least a week after mating.

False pregnancies can occur. The cat that has been sent away to stud but not successfully mated may show every sign of being in kitten with the swelling of her flanks, and even the nipples may turn pink. As the date of kittening approaches, however, the swelling vanishes and the cat returns to her normal size, with no kittens appearing. It is also possible for a frustrated female to have a false pregnancy, although she may never have been near a male cat. The signs are identical; she may go so far as to choose a place to have the imaginary kittens, making a nest in a box or drawer, frequently tearing up paper there. Such females have been known to catch a baby rabbit and take it to the box to mother.

Once it is realized a cat is in kitten, she should be treated normally and never mollycoddled. Her diet should be varied and toward the end it is better not to give very large meals but rather to give several small meals. Well before the kittens are due, the cat should be given a box, lined with newspaper, in a corner away from any drafts and bright lights. However, she may decide that she would prefer to have her kittens in a drawer or on the armchair cushions, and will have to be watched.

Once the kittens have arrived, most cats settle down with them happily suckling, but trouble may start when a cat has only one kitten, as the milk supply is inclined to dry up. Several kittens in the litter, all feeding away, help to increase the milk flow, so that when the mother cat has been away from her kittens for a while she begins to feel uncomfortable and will return to the family quickly for them to feed. With only one, probably using the same nipple all the time, the milk soon dries up in the other nipples, and the mother cat no longer feels the need to return quickly to feed the solitary kitten. The kitten must be encouraged to suck to keep the flow of milk going, and the mother must be watched to make sure that she does not leave the kitten alone for too long. It is better to make the kitten feed from its mother rather than to give it supplementary feeding, as this will make it less inclined to take the mother's milk and will not help the supply. However, this does not always happen, as a mother cat left with only one kitten is inclined to keep close to it all the time.

Until a cat has a first litter, it is difficult to know what kind of mother she will be. She may be very possessive, resenting other cats even looking at her kittens, and disliking the handling of them, even by her owner. On the other hand, another female will purr with delight when her family is looked at and admired. It is advisable to watch her reaction and to treat the kittens accordingly. Sometimes an apparently healthy kitten will be found dead in a corner of the box, almost flattened. Usually, close examination will reveal that the kitten has some physical defect, such as a cleft palate or a twisted back leg. The mother cat, realizing this, deliberately kills the malformed kitten.

Occasionally, a cat may have her kittens quite naturally, will seem well, but by the morning they will have vanished, eaten by her. It is difficult to understand why this should happen. It may be due to a fright or some emotional upset connected with the birth. Fortunately, it is comparatively rare and the majority of female cats make excellent mothers, happy and content, tending their families well.

If the litter is large, weaning should be started when

the kittens are three to four weeks old. This should be done gradually so that they are on a mixed diet until about the age of eight to nine weeks, when they are taking very little milk from their mother. The mother may tend to become spiteful toward the kittens. if they are allowed to suckle for too long. Their sharp little teeth may bite her nipples, causing her intense pain, and she may react accordingly. As happens quite frequently, too, the cat may come into season again, sometimes only a week or two after the kittens are born. As we have seen, it is quite possible for her to be mated again, so she must be watched carefully. When calling, she may become annoyed with the kittens, and her milk may fall off slightly, but it should return in a day or so. During this time it may be necessary to supplement the kittens' feed with a baby food or suitable animal milk food.

If a kitten is eventually to become a stud, he should be chosen with care. Temperament is most important. A cat that is wild and spiteful will make a very poor stud, possibly attacking the female rather than mating. Upbringing is very important, too, with daily handling. He must be groomed regularly and shown as much affection as possible. A stud leads a lonely life, which is a great pity, as the majority of them are very gentle and show great affection toward their owners.

A male kitten can live in the home for about six months, but after that time he should be put outside for a short period each day in a specially built house with a run, with the time being gradually increased until he is used to being alone. By the age of nine months he should be sleeping outside. It is unkind to bring him up as a pet, playing with and nursing him all the time, and then the moment he starts to spray, banishing him outside. A male may be very noisy when he is on his own, missing the companionship of the owner, so his house should be sited where he is able to see people and not feel completely cut off.

No one should keep a stud unless he can provide him with a large stud house and as big a run as possible, to enable him to get sufficient exercise. The stud should also be allowed out under supervision for a certain time each day. It is unwise to allow him complete freedom, as he may pick up an infection and will certainly mate any stray female cat and may even wander away.

When the breeding season is over and no females are being accepted for mating, sometimes it has been found that the male cat will not spray around, and so it is possible to have the cat in the house during the evenings. However, the cat should be carefully watched.

Cat Psychology

Although cats are animals and should always be treated accordingly, it is intriguing to notice that situations arise with them which are similar to human situations.

A cat can become exceedingly jealous of another over a relatively small thing, such as sleeping on a particular favorite cushion. The resentment may build up gradually until it reaches the fighting stage. Even when the bone of contention is removed, the feud may still continue, and careful watching is necessary to make sure the cats do not do serious damage to one another. This sort of thing can start a gang warfare, with all the cats in the household ganging up on the unfortunate one. For example, a cat which had lived and slept peaceably with other cats was sent away to stud. On her return, although she had been away for only three days, her companions refused to accept her and she had to be kept apart for the remainder of her days, living to a ripe old age.

Yet some cats strike up a lifelong friendship with one particular cat. They will always be together, being miserable when separated. Should one of the pair die, the other may be miserable, inconsolable, almost pining away. The introduction of a new kitten may help in this case.

Boredom can cause difficulties. A cat may appear to be very depressed, losing interest in everything around it, and develop unusual habits. It may sit and suck the end of its tail until it is almost raw; it may engage in wool-sucking or wool-eating, often making holes in its owner's cardigan and, given the opportunity, may wash itself almost continuously. If a cat is left alone for long periods, boredom or loneliness may cause it to wander away from home to seek companionship.

Jealousy in a cat can cause psychological problems which need careful handling, particularly if it is caused by a new arrival in the home, be it another cat, a dog or a child. To show disapproval, a hitherto clean cat may become dirty in the house, or may sit and sulk, and even refuse to eat its favorite food. A gentle cat may turn spiteful and be resentful of any attention given to the newcomer.

Usually older cats will accept young kittens or puppies without too much trouble. There may be the occasional swearing when the newcomer walks by, but it rarely develops into anything more. If an owner is careful to make an extra fuss over the resident cat and, at first, feeds the animals separately, by the end of a week they should accept one another. A bouncy puppy should be watched carefully when with the cat in case it gets its eyes clawed, but a big dog will usually settle down quickly with a small kitten, provided the owner has plenty of patience and does not leave them alone together until he is sure that they are friendly.

For some cats, human contact is a necessity, and it is essential for the white cats with blue eyes that sometimes suffer from deafness. For many years this fact was not appreciated, and it was thought that these cats were not very bright. In 1876, Gordon Stables, in his book, *The Domestic Cat,* writing on "The Merits of the White Cat," said, "A pet; gentle and loving above a cat of any other colour, though at times dull, and cross and wayward; given to moods of melancholy." Most cats love the sound of the human voice and will respond accordingly, carrying on a conversation as far as they can. This is impossible for a deaf cat and touch is therefore most important.

It is possible to have a deaf white cat as a pet, and it should make a most attractive and affectionate companion if given the proper training. A deaf cat should not be allowed complete freedom if living on a busy thoroughfare as, unable to hear the traffic, it may be involved in an accident. This problem can be overcome by completely fencing in the garden, thus enabling the cat to go in and out of the house as it pleases. Communication can be established by tapping on the ground: the cat soon learns that the vibrations it feels mean that it is wanted, and responds accordingly. In time, too, hand signals can be recognized and readily understood, a beckoning finger meaning "dinnertime," a pointed finger, a stern "no." A deaf cat particularly loves being nursed and fussed over, adores being stroked and will play eagerly with small toys. It seems to have an extra sense and soon develops an almost complete understanding with its owner.

Like humans, cats differ very much in their personalities, each being an individual. There is the aggressive type which, having been frustrated as a kitten, hits out at any other cat when thwarted. There is the amiable, friendly type, happy and placid, never put out by anything. Another is the fussy housewife type, rarely still, doing everything in a rush, giving herself a hasty lick, then dashing off to see if her kittens are all right, waking them up if they are sound asleep, feeding them for a few minutes, washing them all over and then departing downstairs, with a look of "never a minute to spare in this house."

There is the "Garbo" cat, who is quite happy to be left alone, sitting quietly, purring happily. But let another cat sit near her and she will use the most unladylike language and retire huffily to a different corner. In contrast, there is the cat that cannot bear to be alone.

Then there is the definitely strong-silent male type, stalking proudly among the females, occasionally condescending to play with his kittens.

There are kittens which are definitely as bad as any small boys, knocking things over, tearing up paper, getting the knitting wool into a terrible tangle, rushing up the curtains and jumping onto the table. However, they are always fun, although they are great time wasters.

The Old Cat

A healthy cat ages almost imperceptibly, and as the years slip by it may come as a shock suddenly to realize that a pet and close companion is thirteen, fourteen or even more years of age. There are few outward signs to indicate the age of a particular cat, and any that there are may differ from one cat to another. A long-haired cat may still have the most beautiful, deep, orange-colored eyes when quite old, while another's eyes will have paled to yellow when it is only ten years old. Few cats go gray with age, and many retain thick glossy coats all their lives.

As with humans, and possibly due to diet, cats lose their teeth at varying ages. A cat of seven or eight years may have lost its front teeth completely, while another of fifteen years will have a brilliant white set, with none missing. If veterinary attention has been lacking over the years, the amount of tartar on the teeth may give some indication as to age, but this is not infallible.

Nowadays, it is difficult to say when a cat is really old. A few years ago twelve years was considered to be quite an age; today, probably because of better care and feeding, pets, in particular, seem to live for sixteen years or more, with twenty, twenty-five and even over thirty years not being unknown. One sign of old age is that a cat may start to go thin, with its sides falling in and its backbone easily felt. Its fur, too, may not be so luxurious if long-haired, and thinner and perhaps slightly sticky if short-haired.

Warmth is essential for the old cat, particularly when the weather is cold. In the summer, many old cats (and young ones, too) love to spend hours basking in the sun, so much so that some owners fear their animals may become dehydrated, but this does not seem to happen. Wet and damp should be avoided and the cat kept indoors in really rainy weather. It should be thoroughly dried if by chance it is caught in the rain, as a chill must be avoided at all cost. A few cats suffer from rheumatism and should never be allowed to sit around outside in the damp. For sleeping a cardboard box or a basket lined with newspaper and an old blanket placed on top, put well away from drafts but accessible, is ideal.

The diet may need careful watching, with several small meals a day being preferable to one or two larger ones. Lack of or decaying teeth may make eating difficult, and all the food given should be light, cut into small pieces or minced, and be easily digestible. It may become necessary to give the old cat very little milk if it suffers from loose bowel movements, but if the cat is very fond of it, just give it a little at a time. Should there be some loss of appetite, cooked minced rabbit, or some other favorite food, may prove tempting. Canned sardines, too, may be appreciated, as they are very easy to eat. If the cat is constipated, regular doses of vegetable or mineral oil should be given. The old cat may become fastidious, and show a marked preference for certain foods, and at that age a little spoiling in that direction can do little harm. There should always be plenty of clean water available for drinking and, in very cold weather, this should be slightly warmed.

If the cat is slow moving and reluctant to go outside, several litter boxes should be provided and put in easy reach, as it is surprising how particular even the oldest cat will be about being clean. Allowances must be made for the more frequent passing of urine.

Daily grooming is still important, but this must be done very gently, as there may be very little flesh on the cat, and the coat, too, may be very thin. Any runniness from the eyes should be wiped away, as should any messiness under the tail, as some cats become lazy about cleaning themselves as they age. The eyesight is not usually affected and, unlike dogs, few cats suffer from cataract; the hearing, too, remains fairly good, unless, of course, the cat happens to be one of the Whites with little or no hearing from birth. The ears should be inspected at regular intervals, to make sure there is no ear mite, frequently referred to as canker. If there is a bad smell from the ears due to this, the veterinarian should be consulted as to the correct treatment.

An old cat can be quite demanding in its requirements. If it feels so inclined, it will insist on sleeping on the most comfortable armchair, often the one favored by its owner, and will resent being moved from it. It may also become jealous of any attention given to another cat in the house.

The cat may become much slower in movement and reaction and should certainly not be allowed out if near busy roads as it ages. If there is a garden, it will probably be quite happy to stay in it, but a few cats seem to know when they are dying and wander away from the house as if seeking some place in which to die. When it occurs, the owner may spend hours searching everywhere for his pet and in the end sometimes never know what has happened.

Sleep periods may become longer and longer. In fact, some old cats almost hibernate for a day or more, so much so that the owner may think that his cat is dying, whereas the next day it will be up bright and early looking eagerly for its breakfast.

Affection becomes even more important to the old cat, and a constant watch should be kept to make sure it is not suffering. When the bowel and bladder movements begin to fail and food is refused, a veterinarian should be asked for his opinion, and his advice, however heartbreaking, followed. If he feels the cat is nearing the end of its days, he should be allowed to put it painlessly to sleep, rather than to allow it to drag on for a week or more, however great the sense of loss will be to the owner.

INDEX

Index